EYEWITNESS
TREE

Blue atlas cedar

Rowan berries and leaves

Weymouth pinecone

Acorns

Apples

Magnolia leaf

Monterey cypress

Willow

Hazelnuts

Victoria plum fruit

Ginkgo leaf

Maple seeds

EYEWITNESS
TREE

Written by
DAVID BURNIE

Ornamental apple
fruit

Lodgepole
pinecones

Ash leaf

Fungus feeding on
decaying wood

Hazelnuts

Moss on
decaying wood

Oak wood

DK

Lawson cypress cones

Wellingtonia cone

Pinecone

Western red cedar leaves

Pear

Japanese maple leaf

DK | Penguin Random House

Editorial team Janice Lacock, Sarah Phillips, David John
Design team Carole Ash, Rebecca Johns, Joanne Little
Managing editors Linda Esposito, Andrew Macintyre
Managing art editor Jane Thomas
Special photography Peter Chadwick, Philip Dowell, and Kim Taylor
Picture research Sean Hunter
Editorial consultants The staff of the Natural History Museum, London

RELAUNCH EDITION (DK UK)
Senior editor Chris Hawkes
Senior art editor Spencer Holbrook
US editor Shannon Beatty
Jacket editor Claire Gell
Jacket designer Laura Brim
Jacket design development manager Sophia MTT
Producer, pre-production Nikoleta Parasaki
Producer Vivienne Yong
Managing editor Linda Esposito
Managing art editor Philip Letsu
Publisher Andrew Macintyre
Publishing director Jonathan Metcalf
Associate publishing director Liz Wheeler
Design director Stuart Jackman

RELAUNCH EDITION (DK INDIA)
Senior editor Bharti Bedi
Project art editor Nishesh Batnagar
Editorial team Sheryl Sadana, Virien Chopra
DTP designer Pawan Kumar
Senior DTP designer Harish Aggarwal
Picture researcher Nishwan Rasool
Jacket designer Dhirendra Singh
Managing jackets editor Saloni Talwar
Pre-production manager Balwant Singh
Managing editor Kingshuk Ghoshal
Managing art editor Govind Mittal

First American Edition, 1988
This edition published in the United States in 2015 by DK Publishing
345 Hudson Street, New York, New York 10014
A Penguin Random House Company

15 16 17 18 19 10 9 8 7 6 5 4 3 2 1
001—280098—Sep/15

Copyright © 1990, 2002, 2008, 2015 Dorling Kindersley Limited
All rights reserved

Published in Great Britain by Dorling Kindersley Limited.

A catalog record for this book is available from the Library of Congress.
ISBN 978-1-4654-3847-8 (Paperback)
ISBN 978-1-4654-3848-5 (ALB)

DK books are available at special discounts when purchased in bulk for sales promotions, premiums, fund-raising, or educational use. For details, contact: DK Publishing Special Markets, 345 Hudson Street, New York, New York 10014 or SpecialSales@dk.com.

Printed and bound in China

A WORLD OF IDEAS:
SEE ALL THERE IS TO KNOW
www.dk.com

Larch cones

Rowan leaf

Young Scotch pinecones

Variegated holly leaf

Vine-leaved maple leaf

Osier leaf

Contents

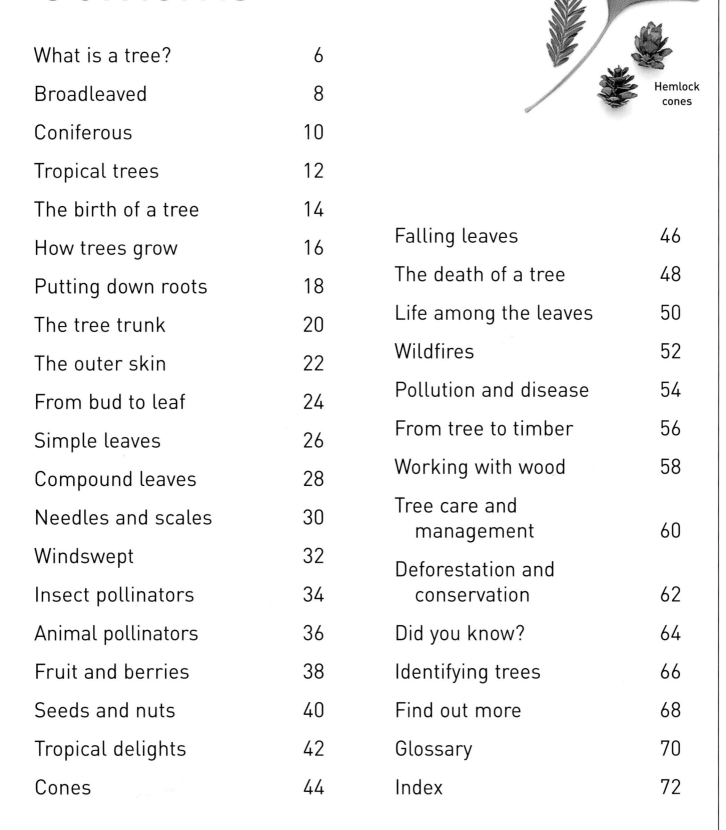

Yew leaves

Hemlock cones

What is a tree?

The earliest plants were smaller than a pinhead. These tiny cells lived in the oceans of the ancient Earth, and, like today's plants, required sunlight to grow. The whole plant kingdom now has evolved to create plants in water and on the land. To flourish, plants needed a way to support themselves: some eventually developed a material called lignin, which made their stems tough and woody so that they could grow taller. The tall plants did better than the small ones, which had to survive in their shade. Eventually, plants with a giant single stem appeared: these were the first trees.

Homage in stone
This is a carved Hindu tree goddess, c.150 CE.

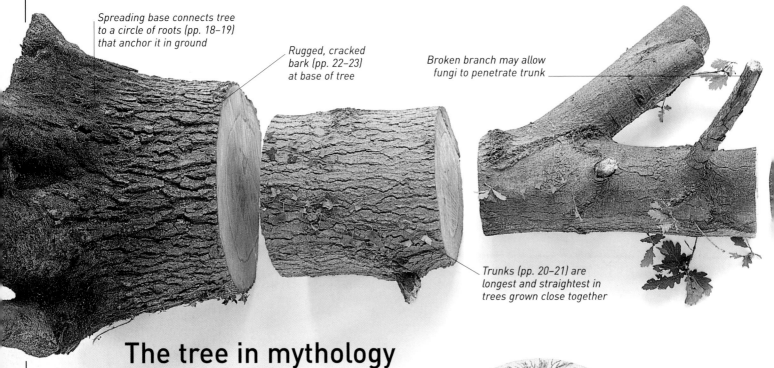

Spreading base connects tree to a circle of roots (pp. 18–19) that anchor it in ground

Rugged, cracked bark (pp. 22–23) at base of tree

Broken branch may allow fungi to penetrate trunk

Trunks (pp. 20–21) are longest and straightest in trees grown close together

The tree in mythology

All over the world, trees have featured in ancient myths, folklore, and rituals. Perhaps because of their size and longevity, many religions have regarded them as sacred symbols, and certain trees have been worshipped as gods: the Druids, for example, worshipped the oak.

Christian belief
The cross on which Christ died was symbolically linked with the tree of life, which grew in the Garden of Eden, and offered everlasting life.

Norse legend
In Scandinavian myths, Yggdrasil is a mighty ash tree that links Earth with heaven and hell. Many legends call it a source of knowledge: the god Odin gained his wisdom by drinking from the spring at its roots.

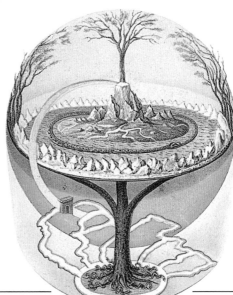

Tree or not?

A tree is a tall plant with a single woody stem. The three main groups of trees are broadleaves (pp. 8–9), conifers (pp. 10–11), and palms (pp. 12–13). Treelike plants also exist, such as bamboo (shown above).

Bark becomes smoother higher up the tree

Each spring, twigs, leaves, and flowers (pp. 32–37) develop from buds (pp. 24–25)

Branches stay at same height above ground as tree grows, becoming thicker each year

Daphne transformed

Greek legend has it that to escape from the amorous Apollo, the goddess Daphne changed into a laurel tree. Today, the laurel has a symbolic use as a token of victory.

In summer, deciduous trees have a dense canopy of leaves, which is shed in winter (pp. 26–31)

Broadleaved

Hedge maple

Vast areas of broadleaved forests have been cleared to make way for fields. Despite this, broadleaved trees, such as oaks, still remain in many places today. Broadleaved trees are so named because most of them have broad, flat leaves. They all produce flowers, and after pollination (pp. 32–37), these flowers develop seeds. Many such trees are deciduous (p. 46)—that is, they shed their leaves every autumn.

Young acorns attached to long stalks

Broadleaved woodland
In natural woodlands, the trees' leaves intercept sunlight and use it to provide the energy they need to grow (p. 16). The woodlands produce huge quantities of wood, leaves, flowers, fruit, and seeds. This generates food for millions of animals, from tiny micromoths (p. 51), to the much larger deer.

Oak in full summer foliage

Oak in winter

The winter sleep
Although most common in warm climates, broadleaved trees can survive in colder regions by shedding their leaves and becoming dormant until spring.

Lichen growing on bark

The oaks
There are about 600 oak species. Some oaks, like the English or pedunculate oak (shown here) are deciduous, while others are evergreen. All oaks are wind-pollinated (p. 32), and all produce acorns.

Young acorns on long stalks

Narrow growth rings

Hard wood, resistant to decay

Leaf litter, rich in decomposing fungi and invertebrate animals

Crooked branches grow at irregular intervals

Different shapes

In windy places, branches on the wind-facing side are killed, so a tree becomes lopsided. A tree growing close to others grows mainly upward as it reaches for light, while a tree in the open forms a leafy crown.

Irregular shape caused by strong winds

A beech growing in an open site

Beeches growing in a plantation

Broad, leathery leaves in clusters at tips of shoots

Growth patterns

Most broadleaved trees have a trunk that grows and divides into many spreading branches of a similar size.

Coniferous

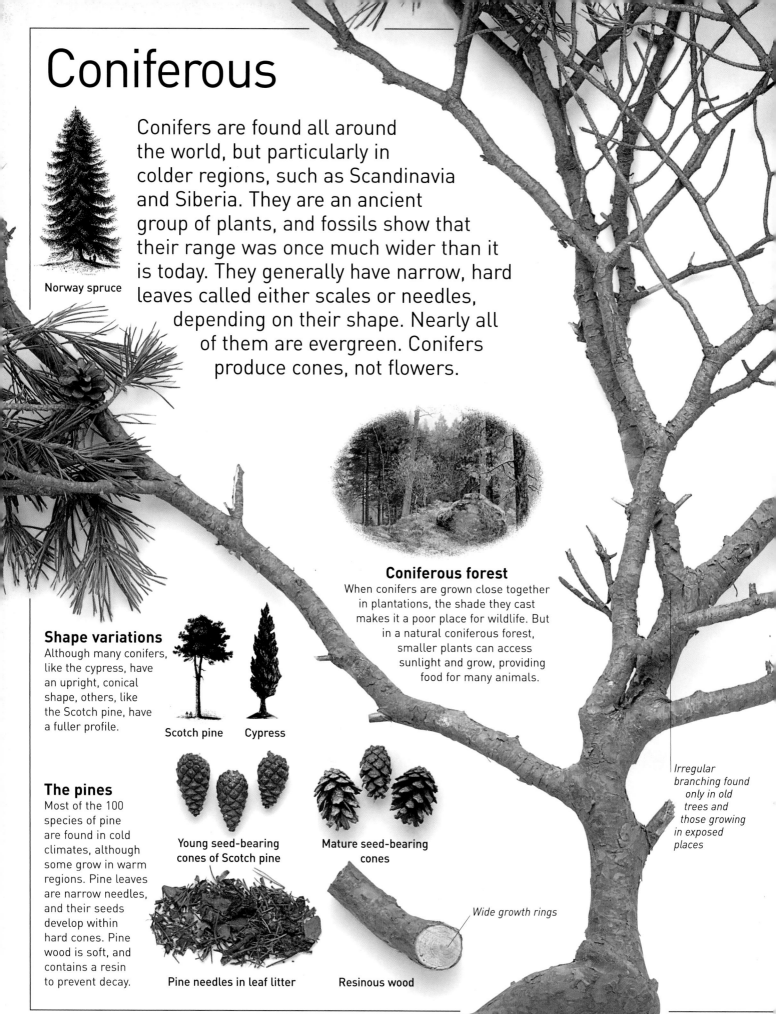

Norway spruce

Conifers are found all around the world, but particularly in colder regions, such as Scandinavia and Siberia. They are an ancient group of plants, and fossils show that their range was once much wider than it is today. They generally have narrow, hard leaves called either scales or needles, depending on their shape. Nearly all of them are evergreen. Conifers produce cones, not flowers.

Coniferous forest
When conifers are grown close together in plantations, the shade they cast makes it a poor place for wildlife. But in a natural coniferous forest, smaller plants can access sunlight and grow, providing food for many animals.

Shape variations
Although many conifers, like the cypress, have an upright, conical shape, others, like the Scotch pine, have a fuller profile.

Scotch pine   Cypress

The pines
Most of the 100 species of pine are found in cold climates, although some grow in warm regions. Pine leaves are narrow needles, and their seeds develop within hard cones. Pine wood is soft, and contains a resin to prevent decay.

Young seed-bearing cones of Scotch pine

Mature seed-bearing cones

Pine needles in leaf litter

Resinous wood

Wide growth rings

Irregular branching found only in old trees and those growing in exposed places

Bark at the top of a mature Scotch pine flakes off in thin, reddish patches

New female cones take almost two years to ripen and shed their seeds

Hard blue-green needles carried in pairs around the sides of the shoots

Christmas trees

The custom of decorating conifers became popular in the 19th century. Other evergreen decorations, however, were used long before the arrival of Christianity: in pagan midwinter festivals, the green foliage of holly or conifers heralded the return of spring.

Conifer growth pattern

Most young conifers have a strong leading shoot, and side branches are thrown out regularly. Later, their growth may become less symmetrical, as this Scotch pine shows.

Tropical trees

Palm

Rain is essential to a tropical tree's growth. In some parts of the tropics, rain falls all year round, allowing broadleaved trees to grow at an extraordinary rate. Area for area, tropical rain forests support the biggest weight of living matter of any land habitat. In places with wet and dry seasons, trees shed their leaves to survive the water shortage. Others, like eucalyptuses, have tough leaves to prevent hot winds drying them out.

Buttress roots
In tropical rain forests, tall trees often compete for sunlight. Where the soil is thin, they may topple over, so some species have evolved buttress roots that spread out and stabilize their trunks.

Beneath the canopy
In tropical rain forests, the unbroken canopy formed by the treetops casts a deep shade on the ground.

Pointed leaves throw off rainwater

Natural drainage
Many tropical trees have leaves with pointed tips, such as this weeping fig. These work like gargoyles on old buildings, throwing off the water in heavy downpours.

Eucalyptuses

Found mainly in the parched outback and subtropical forests throughout Australia, eucalyptuses are some of the fastest-growing trees in the world.

Island jungle

This tangle of vegetation is typical of the northern Australian rain forest. It is home to tree-ferns, which look like palms, but are unrelated to them.

Tree-fern

Leaves unfold like fans as they grow

Eucalyptus leaves contain oil, and attract koalas (p. 51)

Single, fibrous unbranched stem

The one-tree forest

The banyan spreads by forming pillar roots, which develop from roots that grow down from the banyan's branches. One banyan in Kolkata, India, has more than a thousand pillar roots!

Each nut is encased in a waterproof, lightweight husk

Roots emerge through husk

The palms

Nearly all of the roughly 3,000 species of palms are found only in the tropics. The coconut palm's nuts float on seawater until they reach land; the "milk" in the nut allows the seed to germinate on dry beaches.

The birth of a tree

Mature beech tree, more than 150 years old, growing in parkland

The first few months of a tree's life are far more dangerous than the decades, or even centuries, that follow. In a good year, a single oak tree will produce about 50,000 acorns, but most of these will be eaten by animals, or fall to places where they cannot grow. Those that do develop into seedlings could be grazed or trampled on by animals, so only a handful will still be alive a year later. All seeds have a store of food that provides energy to keep them alive, and to fuel growth. Germination—the real birth of the tree—begins in the spring when the days grow warmer.

5 Shedding the case
Fourteen days after germination, the two seed leaves, or cotyledons, expand. Previously folded inside the seed, they now shed the case, and the seed leaves can start to provide the seed with energy.

4 Growing up
Five days after germination, the developing stem has lifted the seed case off the ground. The rootlets start to branch out just below soil level.

Seed case forced off by seed leaves

Emerging seed leaves

Seed case

Stem

Stem

Soil level

Rootlets

Main root

Main root

Rootlets

Seed case curling back

Three-sided seed attached to case

Crack caused by swelling embryo

Seed case

Seed case

Emerging root

1 The fall to earth
The beech tree produces its seeds, also called beechmast or beechnuts, in woody cases. The tree grows a heavy crop in "mast years," which occur about one year in three. Some seeds drop right away; others fall to the ground attached to the case.

2 Germination begins
During the winter months, many of the seeds under a beech tree are eaten by squirrels, mice, finches, and jays. The remaining seeds germinate in early spring. The first sign of life is a crack in the seed's hard shell as the embryo inside it begins to expand.

3 Getting a grip
The developing embryo needs a firm foothold in the ground. A root appears from the pointed end of the seed and grows directly downward. It collects water and minerals from the soil and anchors the seed.

6 Reaching for light

The twentieth day after germination, the seedling with a shoot is tipped by its first true leaves. With luck, this shoot will eventually become the trunk of a mature tree; but if the seedling is under the deep shade of its parent, the young leaves may be starved of light, and the seedling will die.

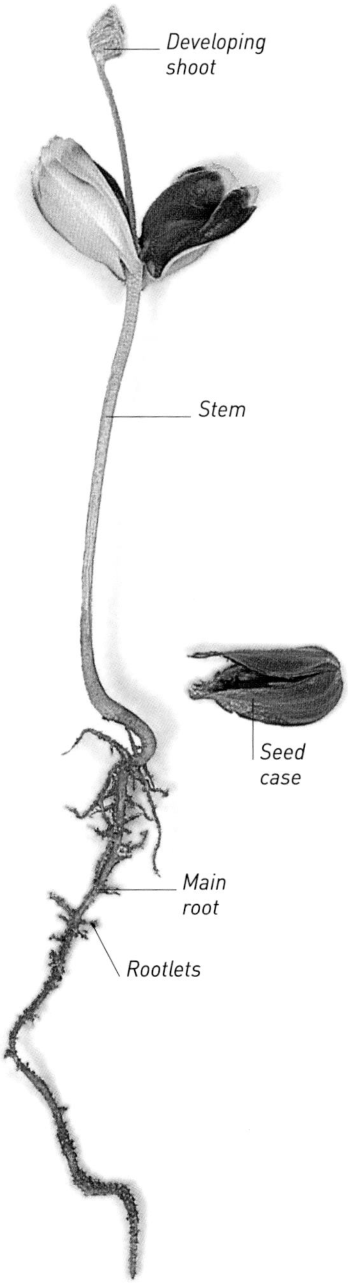

7 Coming into leaf

A month after germination, the stubby seed leaves are still powering the seedling's growth, but the first true leaves are growing. Below ground, the root system has become much more extensive.

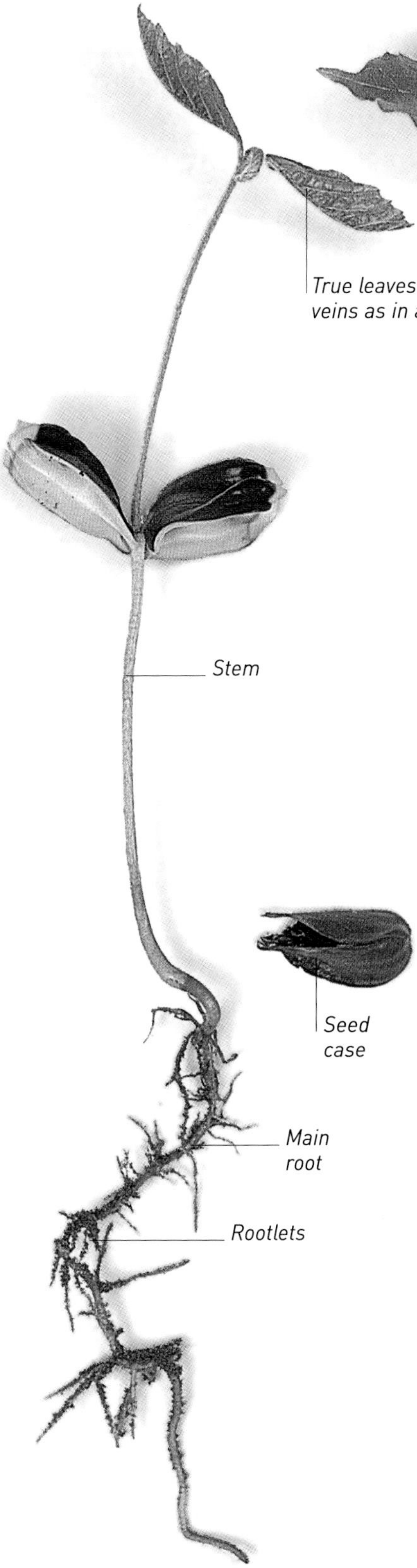

8 The seedling In summer

Fifty days after germination, the seedling has completed most of the growth that it will make in its first year.

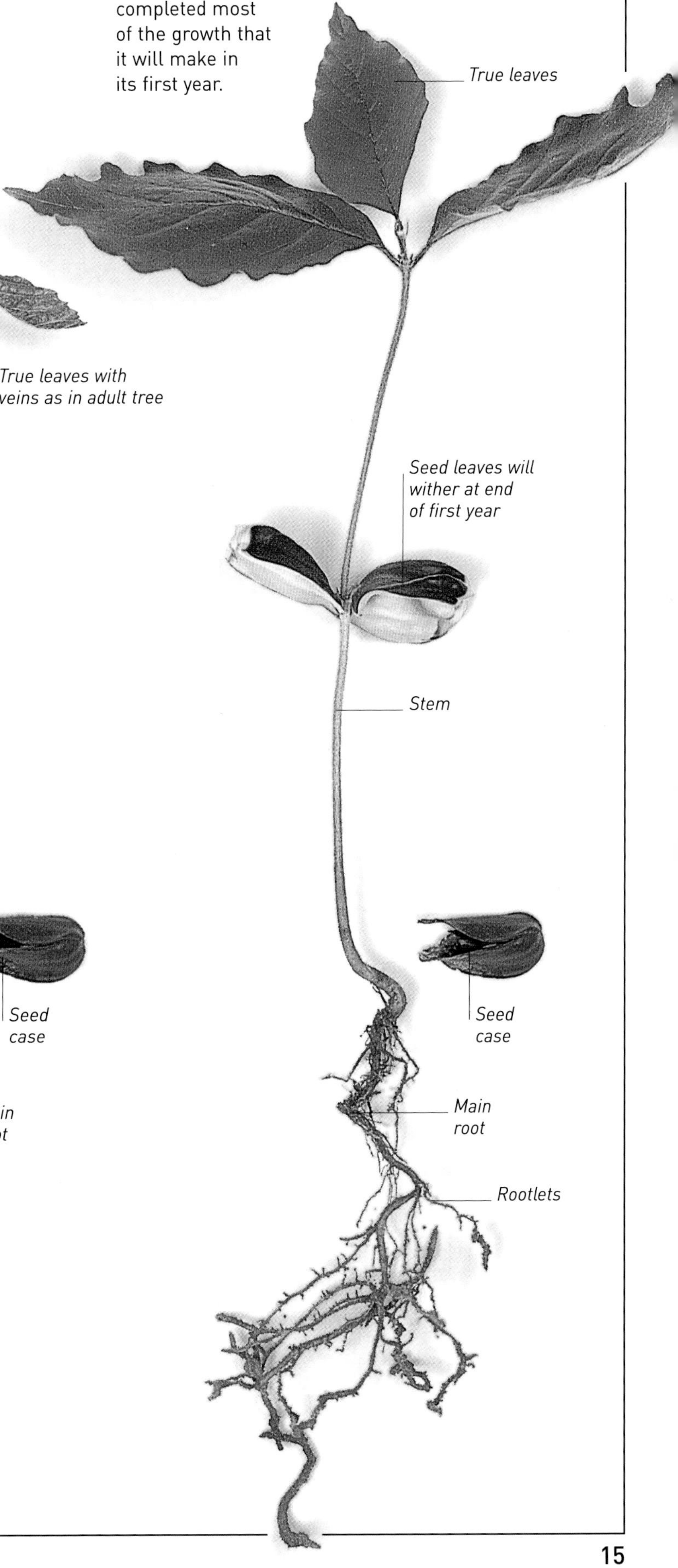

True leaves

Developing shoot

True leaves with veins as in adult tree

Seed leaves will wither at end of first year

Stem

Stem

Stem

Seed case

Seed case

Seed case

Main root

Main root

Main root

Rootlets

Rootlets

Rootlets

How trees grow

Trees grow in two different ways. At the tip of every twig there is a group of specialized cells. When these cells divide they make the twig grow longer, which makes trees grow taller. At the same time, the cambium (a layer of cells that covers the woody part of the tree) produces a different kind of growth. As the cells in the cambium divide, the trunk, branches, twigs, and roots grow fatter. The girth of most mature tree trunks increases by around 1 in (2.5 cm) every year.

A living skin
Despite losing its heartwood, this ash tree survives, as the sapwood transports water and sap.

Hidden strength
The strength of a tree's expanding roots is tremendous. This tree in Cambodia is slowly breaking up the old temple wall on which it grows.

The heaviest trees
Wellingtonias and Californian redwoods grow on mountainsides watered by fog that rolls in from the Pacific Ocean. With few strong winds, the trees' growth is unhindered and they can grow extremely tall.

Heartwood is composed mostly of dead cells

Sapwood is composed of living cells

Bark

Sapwood is composed of living cells

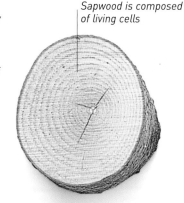

Slow growth
This branch from a yew tree is 75 years old. Its growth rings are packed closely together.

Fast growth
Only about 15 years old, this branch is from a maple tree. Its growth rings are widely spaced.

Ground-huggers
Trees cannot grow in the harsh Arctic tundra, but some shrubs, like this dwarf willow, flourish.

Area of rapid growth

Area of slow growth

Sap stain in partially seasoned wood

Ancient trees
Bristlecone pines are among the oldest living things on Earth, up to 6,000 years old. Found at high altitude in the Rocky Mountains, their growth is extremely slow.

Bark

Lopsided growth
Off-center growth rings like this can be produced in two different ways. First, if a tree grows in an exposed place, its wood grows faster on the side facing away from the wind. Second, with large branches, faster growth often occurs on the underside to help support the weight of the branch.

The growth cycle

For a few weeks every year in temperate-region trees, the growth produced by the cells at the tips of branches is very rapid. So, too, is the growth of leaves as they expand after emerging from their buds (p. 24). The growth in a tree's girth is less noticeable, but it is just as important. The trunk, branches, and roots can only grow longer at their tips, not farther back, which means that once a branch has grown out from the trunk, it will always be at the same height above the ground. And as the trunk can only get fatter, not longer, it cannot lift the branches upward as the tree ages.

New leaves grow every year

Twigs grow longer at their tips

Trunk and branches grow thicker every year

Roots grow longer at their tips and produce root hairs every year (p. 19)

Roots grow thicker every year

Sapwood

Heartwood

Growth ring produced every year

Medullary ray carries nutrients inward

Cambium is the region of growth

Bark

Sapwood is composed of living cells

Heartwood is composed mostly of dead cells

A century of growth

This trunk from a giant sequoia is about 100 years old. The girth of this species can increase by up to 3 in (8 cm) every year.

Narrow rings show that growth was slower here

Wide rings show that growth was rapid here

Fibrous bark made up of dead cells

Putting down roots

As a tree grows, badgers dig new tunnels, creating a denlike home—or sett—among the spreading roots.

Most of a tree's roots grow outward, forming a crisscrossing net that anchors the tree into the ground. The roots of a tree 165 ft (50 m) tall are likely to reach no more than 8 ft (2.5 m) into the ground, but they may spread outward to a distance that matches the tree's height. Over all this ground, tiny root hairs collect water and minerals and channel them into rootlets. The precious water passes from the rootlets into the main roots, and finally into the trunk.

Waterlogged ground

Most trees are unable to grow in ground that is permanently waterlogged because the soil is soft and unstable. It is also very low in oxygen, which tree roots need. But a few trees can live in these conditions, such as mangroves, which are tropical trees that grow on coastal mudflats. They have two special kinds of roots: stilt-roots that arch from the mangrove's trunk and anchor the tree in mud; and breathing roots that grow up through the mud and are exposed to the air at low tide, which enables them to collect oxygen.

Mangrove swamp
On some tropical coasts, mangroves form bands of vegetation that are many miles long.

Coming up for air
The swamp cypress flourishes in the bayou country of the southern United States. It has two unusual characteristics—its knobbly breathing roots, and the fact that it is a deciduous conifer.

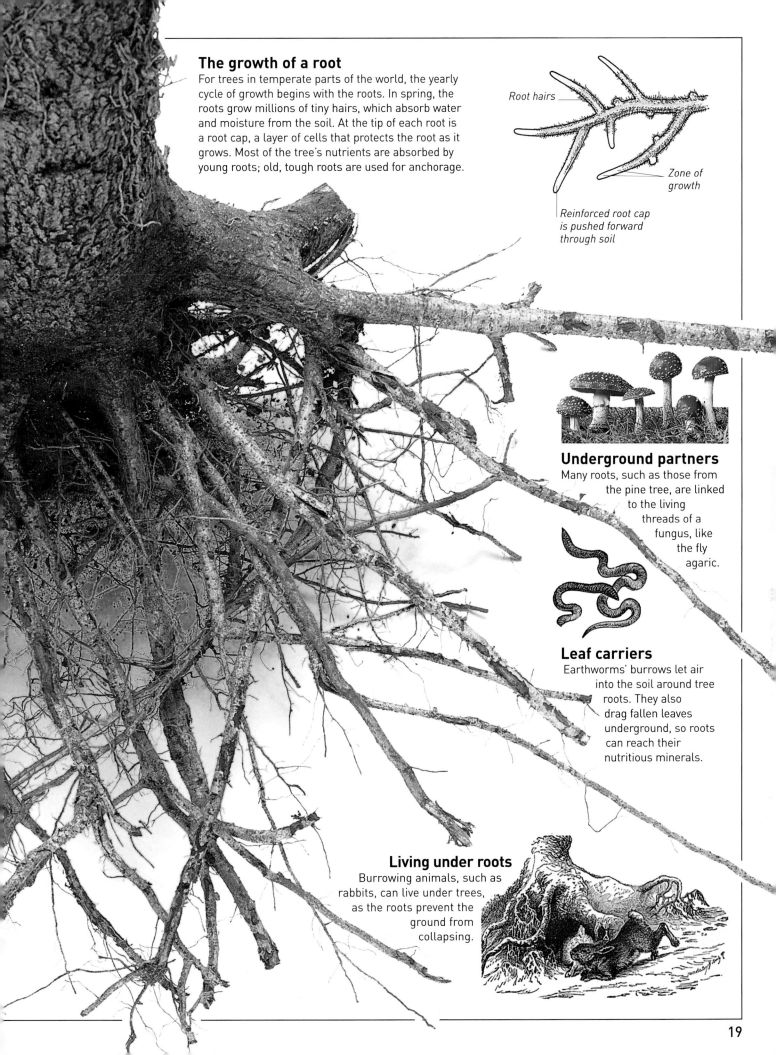

The growth of a root

For trees in temperate parts of the world, the yearly cycle of growth begins with the roots. In spring, the roots grow millions of tiny hairs, which absorb water and moisture from the soil. At the tip of each root is a root cap, a layer of cells that protects the root as it grows. Most of the tree's nutrients are absorbed by young roots; old, tough roots are used for anchorage.

Root hairs

Zone of growth

Reinforced root cap is pushed forward through soil

Underground partners

Many roots, such as those from the pine tree, are linked to the living threads of a fungus, like the fly agaric.

Leaf carriers

Earthworms' burrows let air into the soil around tree roots. They also drag fallen leaves underground, so roots can reach their nutritious minerals.

Living under roots

Burrowing animals, such as rabbits, can live under trees, as the roots prevent the ground from collapsing.

The tree trunk

Bird's nest in a tree

Just below the surface of a trunk, invisible sap draws minerals up from the ground and carries nutrients downward from the leaves (p. 17). The tree guards this pathway for food with its tough bark. Even so, insects, fungi, and parasitic plants sometimes breach this barrier. Nourished by this food, these animals form the base of the tree-trunk food chain.

The spiral creeper
Treecreepers are small mouse-colored birds that feed on tree-trunk insects. Uniquely, they climb each trunk by spiraling around it.

Woodpeckers may excavate and nest in a hole in dead wood

The living pantry
A number of mammals, such as squirrels, take away tree seeds and bury them. But they do not find all their stored seeds, and many germinate. The acorn woodpecker of southwestern America stores acorns in trees or telephone poles.

Acorns in pine bark

Acorn woodpecker

Green coloration on bark caused by a thick layer of minute single-celled plants called algae, which reach the trunk by wind-blown spores

Living bark growing over dead heartwood

Fruiting bodies of fungus has infected damp wood

Life on the trunk
This is a mature maple's trunk. Fungi and insects will attack dead wood, but the tree will survive if living wood supplies water to the leaves.

"Eye" in bark is the scar left by a young branch

Nuthatch and young

Tree-trunk acrobats

Small birds, like the nuthatch, can support their weight while clinging on to a vertical tree trunk. Their agility enables them to collect insects that live in bark crevices. Many of these birds fly from tree to tree, working their way upward as they quickly scan the trunk for food.

Cross-section of nuthatch nest

Bark ruined by squirrels in search of sap

Safety in a tree

Some birds nest in tree-trunk holes and adapt the entrance size and shape by adding mud to it. Tree hornbills have a unique method: the female seals the entrance with a mixture of mud and saliva, leaving just a small hole so that her mate can feed her. The mud entrance dries to become very hard, preventing predators from breaking in.

Healthy side-branch with complete bark covering

Side galleries excavated by growing larvae

Eggs laid at intervals along main gallery

Main gallery excavated by mother beetle

Bark beetle galleries

Pine weevil

Bark beetles

Insect miners

Young bark beetles excavate galleries as they eat through the wood.

Wood borers

Adult weevils use their long snouts to chew and damage tree shoots.

Passengers and parasites

Trees often play host to small, harmless plants, such as mosses, lichens, and ferns in temperate regions, while in the tropics they are joined by flamboyant orchids and bromeliads. More threatening is the mistletoe: its sticky seed is scraped off a bird's beak onto the host tree's bark and produces a root that grows into the living wood. The parasitic mistletoe then extracts nutritious sap from the tree.

The outer skin

A tree's bark protects the tree from attack by animals and fungi, from drying out, and, in some cases, from forest fires. Bark is made up of two layers: the inner layer, called the bark cambium, consists of living cells, but when they die they become the outer bark and form a highly effective barrier against the elements.

Rubber tapping
Certain trees produce white latex, which is collected in the bark to produce rubber.

Bark from an ash sapling

How bark ages
The bark of an ash sapling starts smooth, but develops many cracks as it matures.

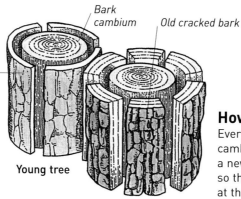

Bark cambium

Old cracked bark

New bark

Young tree

Mature tree

How bark grows
Every year, the bark cambium produces a new layer of bark, so the oldest bark is at the outside of a tree.

Bark from a 60-year-old ash

Oak bark is a natural cork

Cork tile

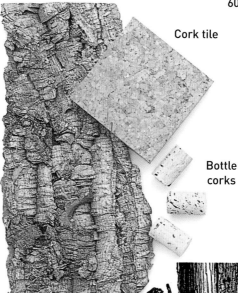

Bottle corks

Thick and thin
The bark of redwoods, like the wellingtonia on the opposite page, can be 1 ft (30 cm) thick. By contrast, the bark of a mature beech tree (left) may be as little as half an inch (1 cm) thick.

Double defense
Old bark, like this from a poplar, is tough and contains chemical defenses. Some trees produce chemicals used in modern medicine.

Stripping cork
Cork is the bark of the cork oak. The outer bark is stripped away to leave the bark cambium, which regenerates new bark.

The past preserved
This piece of hazel bark is about 4,000 years old. The tree that produced it grew in a marsh nearby, and after it died became covered by peat. Acids in the peat, and the lack of oxygen, prevented it from decaying.

Resisting decay
The bark of birch is so durable that the North American paper birch was used by American Indians to make canoes.

Irregular cracking
The horse chestnut (below) has bark that is smooth in a young tree, but that cracks and splits into small, irregular plates as the tree grows.

Maple syrup
The early settlers in the United States made syrup from the sugar maple. Sap was collected by pushing a tube through the dead bark to the sap-conducting layer. The sap was then boiled until just the syrup remained.

Perfumed bark
Made from trees in India and Sri Lanka, cinnamon sticks are produced by cutting bark off saplings; when left to dry, the bark curls up.

Trapped in time
About 50 million years ago, these insects became stuck in this pine resin; fossilized resin is called amber.

The firefighter
The bark of wellingtonia is thick and fibrous, and because it lacks resin it does not easily catch fire, protecting it from forest fires.

Deep crack

Ivy

Breathing through bark
All plants "breathe" through their stems as well as their leaves. This cherry wood (below) shows the enlarged pores that allow gases to penetrate through to the wood beneath.

Flaking bark
Many conifers, such as this yew, have old bark that flakes off in small pieces as the tree grows; the new, red bark is underneath.

Enlarged pores, or lenticels, through which the tree "breathes."

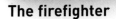

From bud to leaf

In tropical rainforests, the climate is ideal for growth all the year round, yet very few trees can grow non-stop. At higher latitudes, growth is stalled every year by the cold and darkness of winter. Winter buds contain the materials a tree needs for rapid growth in spring. They can be found on all deciduous broadleaved trees and on many conifers. In some trees, the buds contain all the cells needed for the following season's growth; in others, they contain just the foundations for the following year, and the cells divide rapidly once the buds have burst.

Horse chestnut buds

Leading bud with scales partly folded back as it begins to burst

Paired lateral buds

Leaf scar

The horse chestnut
Each of the horse chestnut's large sticky buds contain the material for an entire season's growth. When the days lengthen in early spring, the coating on the bud melts, and the protective scales spring back. The cells within the bud expand rapidly, and in the space of two weeks, the shoot can grow up to 18 in (45 cm). The leading buds—the ones at the tip of a shoot—contain tightly packed flowers and leaves, while the lateral buds (the ones on the sides of the branches) contain only leaves.

Immature leaves

Bud scales

Immature stem

Inside a bud
A bud contains immature leaves folded inside a protective case.

One year ago
Last year's growth extends from the leading bud back to the girdle scar.

One-year-old side shoot formed from lateral bud at tip of twig

Dormant buds begin to grow only if the growing buds are damaged

Girdle scar shows where one season's growth ended and the next began

Three-year-old side shoot formed from lateral bud at tip of twig

Girdle scar

Two years ago
The twig made a relatively small increase in length and did not produce any side shoots.

Three years ago
During this year, the twig did not grow very much. The twig produced a side shoot, which is now three years old.

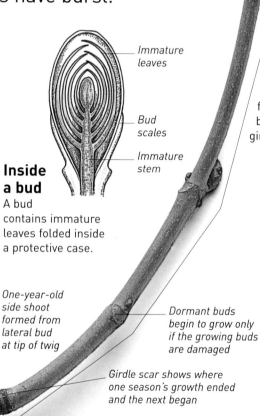

"Witch's brooms"
Infections may cause uncontrolled bud growth, often seen in birches.

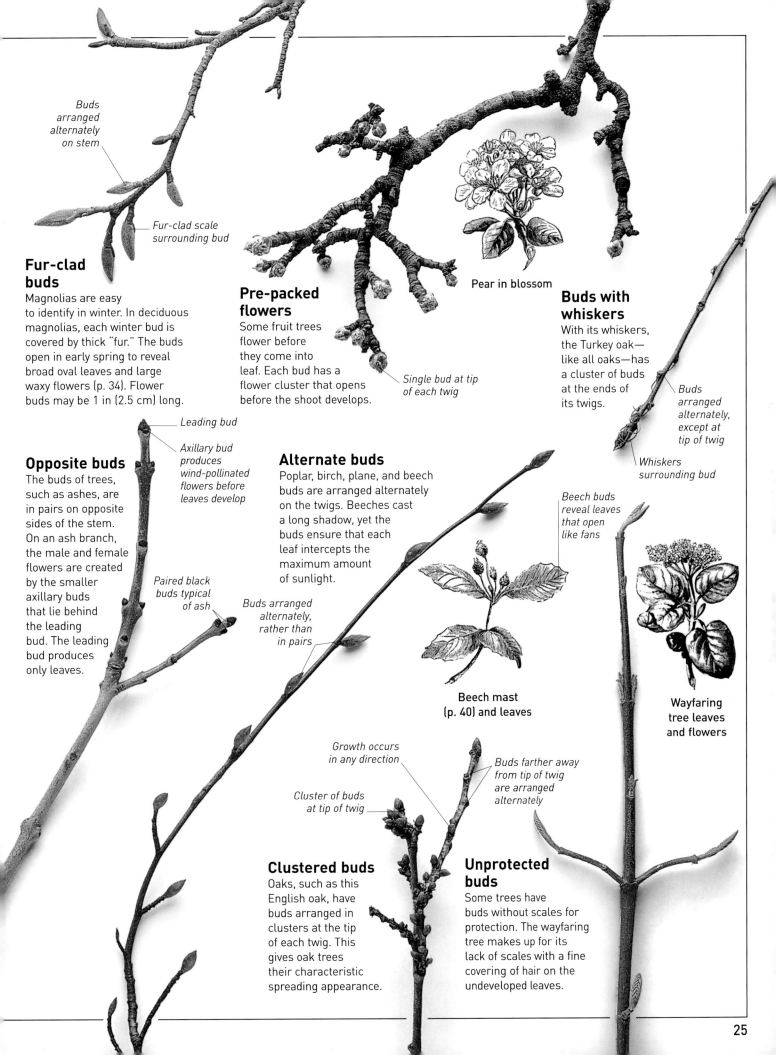

Fur-clad buds

Buds arranged alternately on stem

Fur-clad scale surrounding bud

Magnolias are easy to identify in winter. In deciduous magnolias, each winter bud is covered by thick "fur." The buds open in early spring to reveal broad oval leaves and large waxy flowers (p. 34). Flower buds may be 1 in (2.5 cm) long.

Pre-packed flowers

Some fruit trees flower before they come into leaf. Each bud has a flower cluster that opens before the shoot develops.

Single bud at tip of each twig

Pear in blossom

Buds with whiskers

With its whiskers, the Turkey oak—like all oaks—has a cluster of buds at the ends of its twigs.

Buds arranged alternately, except at tip of twig

Whiskers surrounding bud

Opposite buds

Leading bud

Axillary bud produces wind-pollinated flowers before leaves develop

The buds of trees, such as ashes, are in pairs on opposite sides of the stem. On an ash branch, the male and female flowers are created by the smaller axillary buds that lie behind the leading bud. The leading bud produces only leaves.

Paired black buds typical of ash

Alternate buds

Poplar, birch, plane, and beech buds are arranged alternately on the twigs. Beeches cast a long shadow, yet the buds ensure that each leaf intercepts the maximum amount of sunlight.

Buds arranged alternately, rather than in pairs

Beech buds reveal leaves that open like fans

Beech mast (p. 40) and leaves

Wayfaring tree leaves and flowers

Clustered buds

Growth occurs in any direction

Cluster of buds at tip of twig

Oaks, such as this English oak, have buds arranged in clusters at the tip of each twig. This gives oak trees their characteristic spreading appearance.

Buds farther away from tip of twig are arranged alternately

Unprotected buds

Some trees have buds without scales for protection. The wayfaring tree makes up for its lack of scales with a fine covering of hair on the undeveloped leaves.

Simple leaves

Leaves take in energy from sunlight and use it to turn carbon dioxide and water into sugars. These sugars can then be used as a fuel, or they can form cellulose, the substance that forms the tree's cells. Leaves of broadleaved trees are either simple or compound (p. 28).

Veins spread out across the leaf blade in a network

Microscopic pores on surface of leaf allow gases to enter

Leaf blade

Midrib

Close-up of a simple broadleaf

Stalk or petiole

Lance-leaved willows
Many willows have long, narrow leaves with silvery hairs on the undersides.

Osier

White willow

Toothed oval leaves
The shape of the cultivated cherry leaf is common.

Jagged teeth around edge of leaf

Upper surface, covered in fine hairs

Young giant
The oval leaves of some magnolias can grow up to 1 ft (30 cm) long.

Saw-toothed chestnuts
The sweet chestnut's jagged, tough leaves are a familiar sight in Europe.

Heart-shaped leaves
Symmetrical heart-shaped leaves are uncommon: the judas tree (above) and katsura have them.

Unequal lobes
In summer, unequal leaves grown by limes often become covered with honeydew made by sap-sucking insects.

Smooth dark upper surface

Underside

Soft undertones
White poplar leaves have downy undersides.

Copper beech descended from a natural mutation

Normal holly

Variegated leaves
In a variegated leaf, the green pigment chlorophyll is reduced or absent in parts. These leaves rarely survive in nature.

Variegated holly

Variegated holly

Unusual pigments
Other pigments mask the green chlorophyll, in dark-colored leaves.

Cultivated Japanese maple

Cultivated Japanese maple

Young leaf emerging from sheath on growing shoot

Central notch divides leaf in two

Two-pointed leaf

Parallel veins

English oak

Variable shapes
Most deciduous oaks have lobed or toothed leaves, which feel leathery. Evergreen oaks have short, lance-shaped leaves.

White oak

Red oak

Odd tree out
The two species of tulip tree— one North American and the other Chinese—have large, flat-ended leaves unlike any other tree. This specimen is a young leaf with two points; large mature leaves usually have four points (p. 37).

Ancient survivor
The primitive ginkgo's fanlike leaves have not changed for more than 200 million years.

Vine-leaved Japanese maple

Handlike leaves
Maple leaves have handlike shapes. However, some species, such as the snake-bark maples of China, Japan, and North America, have scarcely lobed leaves. The leaves of another maple, the box elder, are compound.

Snake-bark maple

Japanese maple

City dwellers
Although plane leaves are hand-shaped, planes are not related to maples, as their fruits (p. 41) show. Plane leaves have a tough, glossy surface that is washed clean by rain, helping them to grow in polluted, city air.

Late into leaf
Catalpas, or Indian bean trees, have some of the largest of all simple deciduous leaves, reaching up to 1 ft (30 cm) in length. Catalapas are natives of the subtropics.

Mature catalpa

Compound leaves

Some of the biggest leaves found on broadleaved trees are compound, and can measure up to 3 ft (1 m) from stalk to tip. They grow from a single bud, and when autumn comes many of them fall off in one piece, leaving a large leaf scar where they were attached to the tree.

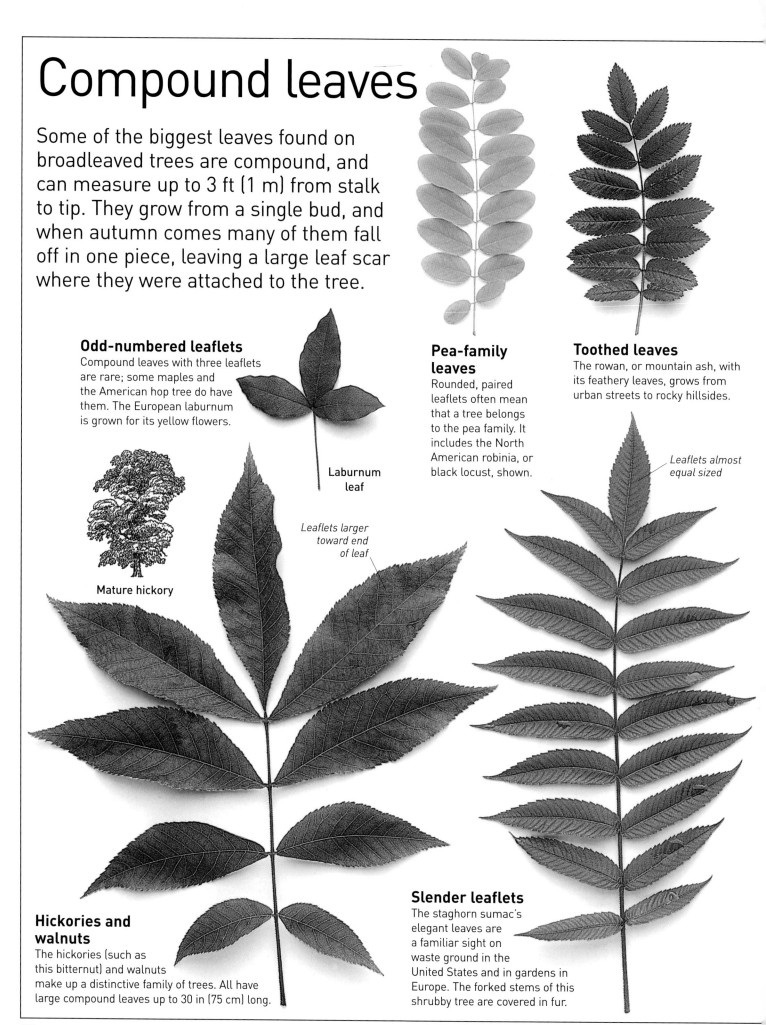

Odd-numbered leaflets
Compound leaves with three leaflets are rare; some maples and the American hop tree do have them. The European laburnum is grown for its yellow flowers.

Laburnum leaf

Mature hickory

Pea-family leaves
Rounded, paired leaflets often mean that a tree belongs to the pea family. It includes the North American robinia, or black locust, shown.

Toothed leaves
The rowan, or mountain ash, with its feathery leaves, grows from urban streets to rocky hillsides.

Leaflets almost equal sized

Leaflets larger toward end of leaf

Hickories and walnuts
The hickories (such as this bitternut) and walnuts make up a distinctive family of trees. All have large compound leaves up to 30 in (75 cm) long.

Slender leaflets
The staghorn sumac's elegant leaves are a familiar sight on waste ground in the United States and in gardens in Europe. The forked stems of this shrubby tree are covered in fur.

Horse chestnut leaf

*Leaflets
arranged
in a circle*

**Mature ash
tree in leaf**

Short-stay leaves

In Europe, the ash is the most common
large tree with compound leaves. In
the autumn, the ash is slow to shed its
foliage. According to folklore, the ash
tree possessed medicinal powers, and it
was believed that a sick child would be
cured if he or she was passed through
the branches of the ash.

Palmate leaves

The leaves of the horse chestnut
family have fingerlike leaflets. The
horse chestnut has seven or nine
leaflets; the North American
buckeyes usually have five.

Hercules club

Doubly divided

The Hercules
club from
North America
has huge leaves
that are twice
compound: each
leaflet is attached to
a side stalk. The
leaves may grow up
to 3 ft (1 m) long and
almost as wide.
Doubly divided
leaves are very
unusual, and only
one tree, the
Kentucky coffee tree
from North America
(though not related
to the true coffee
bush), is common.

*Leaflets paired
and of equal size*

29

Needles and scales

The needles and scales of conifers are quite unlike the leaves of broadleaved trees. They have parallel veins and a hard or leathery surface. With a few exceptions, such as larches, they remain on the tree all year. Including the yews, there are seven families of conifers; the most important are the pines, redwoods, and cypresses. The pine family also includes firs, spruces, cedars, and larches. Conifers have a variety of leaf shapes.

Ornamental conifers

Specially bred conifers can have green, yellow, or even blue foliage. These scales are from a sawara cypress.

Blue atlas cedar

Blue-green needles of cultivated blue atlas cedar

Needles in pairs

Rosettes

Many conifers are cedars, and can be identifed by their evergreen needles that grow in rosettes.

Scotch pine

Arolla pine

Needles in fives

Needles in bunches

Pines have long needles, which grow in bunches of two, three, or five. Each needle has a thick outer layer, or cuticle, and a coating of wax to reduce water loss.

Monterey pine

Needles in threes

Flat, dark green needles

Graveyard sentinel

Often planted in graveyards, toxic yews are a symbol of death.

For all seasons

Firs have tough, flat leaves to cope with heavy snow. Their sloping branches and smooth, flexible leaves shed snow easily. The leaves have a built-in "antifreeze" and are not damaged by frost.

Underside of silver fir

Many fir leaves are differently colored above and below

Upper side of silver fir

Hard, triangular leaves with spiked tips

Monkey puzzle

New needles

Old needles

The coppicing conifer
The Californian redwood produces sprouts from its stump after felling, just as in a coppiced broadleaved tree (p. 61).

Needles on pegs
Spruces have spiky needles that grow from small "pegs" on their twigs. Christmas trees are usually Norway spruces.

Scales around the stem
The Japanese cedar (actually a redwood) has small, scalelike leaves around its stems.

Unique appearance
The monkey puzzle, or the Chile pine, is actually not a pine, but one of an unusual family of conifers found mainly in South America and Australia.

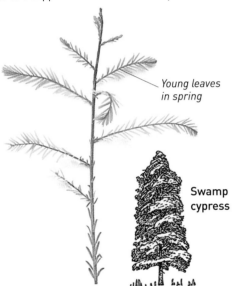

Young leaves in spring

Swamp cypress

Soft, flexible needles are shed every autumn

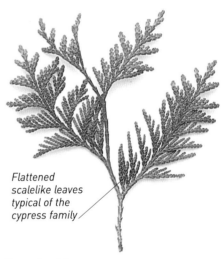

Flattened scalelike leaves typical of the cypress family

Bursting into leaf
The swamp cypress (p. 18) is a deciduous redwood. Their leaves are yellowish in spring, but become green as they mature.

The deciduous conifer
Larches can grow in the coldest climates. Like cedars, they have needles in rosettes.

Scented leaves
Thujas are members of the cypress family. The western red cedar is a thuja. When its leaves are crushed, they smell of pineapple.

Out of the east
The dawn redwood's feathery foliage is also known from fossils. It was thought to be extinct until discovered growing in China in the 1940s.

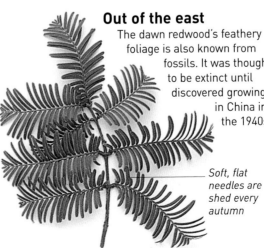

Soft, flat needles are shed every autumn

A contrast in scale
Although the wellingtonia, or giant sequoia, is one of the world's biggest trees, it has some of the smallest leaves. Its tiny scales are packed tightly around the stems.

Two types of leaves
Some junipers have spiky leaves when young and scalelike leaves when adult. The common juniper, shown here, only has spiky leaves.

Windswept

Tree flowers grow in a huge range of shapes and sizes. All broadleaved trees produce true flowers, while conifers grow simpler structures that are not flowers in the strict sense of the word. Many trees rely on the wind to transfer male reproductive cells, or pollen, to the female cells.

Leaves sprouting

Female "flower"

Male "flower"

Exposed to the wind
All coniferous trees are wind-pollinated. In the Lawson cypress, male "flowers" develop at the branchlets' tips, so the pollen can catch the wind.

Flowers first
Larches shed their pollen in early spring. The female "flowers" that develop into woody cones contain the seeds (p. 44).

Male "flowers" on underside of twig

Male "flowers" (catkin)

Individual male flower within catkin

Sticky stigma traps pollen floating in air

Anther

Hazel catkin
Catkins form in the autumn, but do not open until the following spring.

Separate sexes
In the yew, the male (shown) and female "flowers" grow on different trees. They develop on the undersides of its twigs in small clusters.

Early flowering hazel
The hazel is one of the first wind-pollinated trees to come into flower in the spring. If it is above freezing for just two or three days, the catkins release their pollen into the air.

Female hazel flowers

Female flowers

Sexes together
The alder has male and female flowers that grow on the same tree.

Young leaf

Male flowers (catkin)

Male flowers (catkin)

The woodland hornbeam
The hornbeam is a tree of deep woodland. Its flowers appear just as the leaves are beginning to sprout.

Wind-blown pollen
In dry weather, alder catkins shed millions of pollen grains into the air, each 0.03 mm across.

Growing shoot

Cluster of male "flowers"

Past clues
Palynologists can learn what trees grew where from pollen preserved in peat deposits.

Cluster of female flowers

Pollen everywhere
Ornamental plane trees shed huge quantities of pollen in spring. Male and female flower clusters hang from the tree in small groups.

Pollen with sails
Pines produce enormous numbers of pollen grains, and if the male "flowers" are given a sharp knock, a cloud of yellow pollen appears. Like a sail, two tiny air-filled sacs attached to the grains carry them through the air.

Cluster of male Scotch pine "flowers"

Straggly catkins
The catkins of the English oak open in late spring. The female flowers produce the acorns and are at the tips of the shoots.

Catkin divided into three branches

Female flowers on stalks, a feature of English oak

Catkin

Branched catkins
Hickories shed their pollen in early summer from catkins that are branched into three. The female flowers, which are at the tips of the shoots, are quite hard to see.

Stigma of female flower

New and old growth
The walnut's catkins sprout from the previous year's shoot. The smaller female flowers, whose sticky stigmas can be seen here, develop at the end of the new shoot.

33

Insect pollinators

Tree flowers pollinated by animals, particularly insects, are the easiest to spot. Insect-pollinated flowers have sugar-rich nectar that draws bees, beetles, and other insects to them. The tiny pollen grains have a sticky coating that makes them stick to an insect's body so that they can be transferred between trees.

Attracting by scent
The bird cherry attracts insects not only by color, but also by smell.

Stigma (female)

Anther (male)

Insects transfer pollen from male anthers to the female ovule via the stigma

Ovule (female)

Flower made up of fleshy scales

After pollination, flowers droop—this clears a path for bees toward unpollinated flowers

Kanzan cherry
The Kanzan Japanese cherry is one of the most popular culivated varieties. Huge clusters of flowers weigh down its branches in spring, but this variety never produces fruit.

An ancient lineage
The first flowers to appear on Earth belonged to magnolia-like plants, and their cuplike blooms have probably changed little in 200 million years.

A wealth of breeding
Japanese flowering cherries may have come from four wild cherry species.

Double ring of petals found only in cultivated varieties

Anthers and stigma reduced in size

Double ring of petals

Ornamental apple
Like all apples, the delicate flowers of this ornamental crab have five petals that sit on a cup known as a receptacle. After the flower has been pollinated by visiting insects, the receptacle swells to produce the fruit.

Ring of five petals

One sex at a time
As in many flowers, the stigma of the sloe, or blackthorn, matures before the anthers release their sticky pollen to prevent the flower from pollinating itself.

Clusters of flowers on spiny side-branches

Encrusting lichen

All mixed up
Pollinated by bees, each flower head of the horse chestnut is made up of a mixture of flower types: some are entirely male, while others have both male and female parts. Only the second type can produce "conkers."

Ripe anthers covered in pollen

Mixed orchards
The flowers of most apple varieties will only produce fruit if they receive pollen from a different variety. For this reason, farmers often plant different varieties together.

Animal pollinators

The flowers of many trees lure animals that distribute pollen in return for a meal of nectar, a sugary liquid produced by the flower. The flowers attract their pollinators by their color and scent, and are shaped so that the animal becomes dusted with pollen.

Each flower has five petals; the lowest pair springs open when an insect lands on it

Spring-loaded
The flowers of the Judas tree are arranged so that the weight of a visiting insect makes them spring open.

Tiny flowers
Maples have clusters of nectar-rich flowers, and each one has a ring of pollen-producing stamens.

Judas tree in flower

Soft landing
Small flowers packed closely together, like those of the rowan, provide insects with a convenient landing platform.

Wild hawthorn

Cultivated hawthorn with double ring of petals

Blaze of color
Hawthorns produce heavily scented flowers. One hawthorn, the Glastonbury thorn, is unusual in that it flowers twice a year.

Bract

Flower

Flower bud

Flower beginning to open with sepals folding back

Circle of six petals

Sepals folded back

False petals

In most flowers it is the large petals that attract pollinators, but some flowers have evolved other ways of getting noticed. This flower (above) is from a North American dogwood. The four structures that look like petals are special leaves called bracts, which help to attract insects.

Showy petals at mouth of flower

Tube leading to nectar

Beak forms a narrow tube for drinking nectar

Named for its shape

The tulip tree gets its name from its cup-shaped flowers, which, like those of the related magnolias, are large and have a central spire.

Bird pollination

In the Americas, hummingbirds pollinate many species of plants, including some trees.

Tubular flowers

The flowers of the catalpa, or Indian bean tree, are shaped so that a visiting insect has to clamber deep inside a tube to reach the nectar. In doing so, it is dusted with pollen.

Hairs at tip of tongue form a brush to collect pollen

Bat pollination

Bat-pollinated trees include the baobab and kapok (p. 43), both of which have big flowers that produce a lot of nectar, especially at night. Bats eat both pollen and nectar, and in doing so transfer pollen from one flower to another on their tongues and noses.

Insect lure

Elder flowers have a powerful smell that insects, especially hover flies, find highly attractive. This flower's perfume can be noticed in elder flower wine.

Fruit and berries

After a tree's flowers have been pollinated, the female part of the flower produces seeds. Trees produce bright, tasty fruit that attracts animals, like birds. In return for a meal, a bird scatters seeds in its droppings, and new trees may spring up where the seeds fall.

Forbidden fruit
The fruit that caused Adam and Eve's fall into sin is often said to be an apple; the Bible just refers to it as a fruit.

Small seed surrounded by a fleshy jacket, known as an aril

Chemical colors
Red berries, like those of the rowan, are colored by carotenoids; they get their name because they also color carrots orange.

Poisonous fruit
Yews, like junipers, are conifers, but, uniquely, they produce juicy, colored "berries." A bird can digest the fleshy aril and the poisonous seed passes through its body intact.

Mythic mulberry
According to Greek legend, the mulberry's fruit was stained red by the blood of the ill-fated lover Pyramus.

Ripening black mulberry

Ripe black mulberry

Silkmoth caterpillars feed only on white mulberry leaves

Mulberries hanging down beneath leaves

Midwinter food
Hawthorn berries are a vital food for birds in winter. They remain on the tree after most other hedgerow berries have disappeared.

The tenacious elder
Elderberries are often eaten by birds. The seeds that fall in their droppings can germinate and grow with almost no soil.

Cultivated fruit

Gardeners have spent centuries adapting fruit to human needs. Wild apples, for example, are small and bitter, and loved by birds, but not by humans. More than a thousand cultivated varieties have been produced, all much larger and sweeter than their wild counterparts. This is done by choosing seeds from promising trees, and crossing one tree with another to get the best characteristics from both.

Science and the apple
Apple breeders, or "pomologists," use the science of genetics to produce apples that taste good and are easy to pick.

The "Worcester pearmain" is a modern variety

Fleshy layer develops around the base of the pollinated flower

Seeds

The "russet" is an old, established variety with a thick, rough skin

Single, hard pit typical of plum fruit

Seed

Pear

Boundary of seed compartment

Nectarine

From pit to fruit
Damsons are easy to grow from their pits. These are some of the smallest cultivated plums.

Out of the wild
Most cultivated plums descend from two shrubs, the sloe, or blackthorn, and the cherry plum.

Family likeness
The plums also include cherries, peaches, apricots, nectarines, and almonds.

Divided up
The seed compartment of apples and pears is divided into sections, each containing one or two seeds.

The citrus fruits
Citrus fruits, like oranges and lemons, contain fruit sugars and citric acid.

Sweet and sour
Oranges originally came from Asia. The sweet orange, used for eating, and the Seville orange, used for marmalade, are two different species.

Seed compartments visible at flat end of fruit

Staple diet
Thrushes, blackbirds, and many other birds rely on berries to survive the winter.

The medlar
Like the apple, the seed compartment of the medlar is divided into five sections. Medlars are usually eaten only when they begin to rot.

The ancient olive
Botanically speaking, the olive is a fruit. Its oil has been cultivated for thousands of years.

Seeds and nuts

Trees disperse their seeds in different ways: some wrap them up in berries that are tempting to birds (p. 38), while others produce seeds inside tough cases. Some trees, like walnuts, produce well-protected seeds that are carried away by mammals, such as squirrels, and, although some seeds are eaten, a number survive and germinate. Other trees have seeds inside winged cases and these are carried by the wind. Some riverside trees use water to disperse their seeds.

Seed catkins
In late summer, wing-nut trees are covered in giant catkins. These are long clusters in flanged cases; the short flanges probably help to dislodge the seeds once ripe.

Filberts

Beech banquet
Annually, beech trees produce mast, an oil-rich seed. In the past, pigs were fattened up with these seeds.

Cobs and filberts
Wild hazelnuts are sold as "cob nuts." The larger filberts come from a hazel that grow in Europe.

Seeds on threads
Each swelling in a cucumber tree splits open to reveal a brilliant red seed suspended on a silklike thread.

Small nuts
Pistachios come from a small Asian tree now grown around the Mediterranean and in the southern United States.

Horse chestnut cases are usually spiny

Prickly case protects developing nuts

Roasting chestnuts

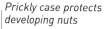

Winter warmer
The best sweet chestnuts grow in warm climates, such as in Spain and California, USA.

Shiny "Conkers"
Horse chestnuts, or "conkers," are slightly poisonous to humans. Other mammals, like sheep, can eat them.

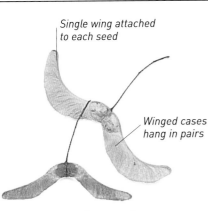

Winged maple seeds

When the maple seed falls inside its case, it spirals to the ground like a miniature helicopter.

Single wing attached to each seed

Winged cases hang in pairs

Seeds are scattered as pods split open

Poisonous seeds

The laburnum tree is often grown in gardens, and has highly poisonous seeds.

Ash keys often remain on tree throughout the winter

Flying keys

Completely female ash trees produce winged "keys;" however, male trees have no keys. In trees with both male and female branches, only the female ones bear keys.

Long clusters of seeds disintegrate during the winter

Lime nutlets

Lime trees have small bunches of yellowish flowers. After these have been pollinated, each flower produces a furry nut containing the seeds.

First arrival

Each birch seed is enclosed in a case with two tiny wings. The fruits are light enough to be blown long distances.

Unripe seed-head

Alder "cones"

Alder seeds develop inside the female catkin. Although unrelated, the mature woody catkin looks like a pinecone.

Ripe acorns of Turkey oak

Healthy unripe acorn

Edible seeds

Most oaks do not begin to produce acorns until they are about 50 years old. To a botanist, acorns are in fact nuts, but they are not commonly called nuts because they are not often eaten.

Acorn cup deformed into "knopper gall" by larva of gall wasp

"Sporting" seeds

The tulip tree's seeds grow in a pointed seed-head. Originally green, the cluster gradually turns brown and opens to look like a shuttlecock.

The squirrel's hidden stores

Many seeds are eaten by squirrels, and others are buried to provide the squirrels' winter stores.

Skin surrounding nut

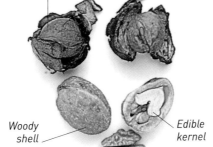

Woody shell

Edible kernel

Colored skins

On the tree, a walnut is covered by a green skin that turns black, collapses, and releases the nut.

American favorite

From North America, the pecan is produced by a tree related to the walnut, and its nuts taste similar.

Hairy irritants

Plane tree seeds grow in ball-shaped clusters, which stay on the tree all winter. In spring they burst open, releasing the seeds and millions of tiny golden hairs.

Tropical delights

Edible fruit and nuts from tropical trees have been bred by man since ancient times. The date palm, for instance, has been cultivated for at least 5,000 years. People have also carried many species from one place to another to provide food. Examples include papaya, avocado, and cocoa, which originally grew in South America, and the mango, which came from Asia.

The coconut palm is a tree that spreads by waterborne seeds

Tamarind pods
The Indian tamarind tree is a member of the pea family (p. 28). The flesh around the seeds is a valuable spice.

Dried nutmeg

The spice trade
Many spices produced from tree seeds are used to flavor food.

Nutmeg and mace
The nutmeg tree provides two spices: nutmeg, which is the tree's seed, and mace, which is the fleshy network that surrounds the seed.

Hard shell protects the nutritious kernel

Seeds and case together weigh up to 3.5 lb (1.5 kg)

Stalk attaches pot to tree

Thick wooden case surrounds nuts

Brazil nut
These nuts come from the Amazonian rain forest. The trees on which they grow have never been successfully cultivated, so all Brazil nuts must be gathered from wild—and often very tall—trees.

Lightweight husk acts as a float

Hole closed by plug

Far from home
Many trees that grow on tropical coasts disperse their seeds, like this *Barringtonia*, by dropping them into the sea, where they are carried off by currents. Many eventually sink, but some do reach land and take root.

Monkey pot nuts

Monkey pot
The "monkey pot" tree produces its seeds in wooden cups that Indians once used for catching wild monkeys.

Plug

Meat tenderizer
The sweet papaya, or pawpaw, is rich in papain. Once extracted from the fruit, it is used to soften meat.

Date palms

The mango
Sweet-tasting mangoes come from trees that originally grew in southeast Asia.

Baobab tree

The shrinking tree
The baobab produces long, sausage-shaped pods packed with seeds rich in vitamin C. The baobab has a huge swollen trunk that stores water. In a drought, the tree shrinks as this water supply is used up.

Coconut germinating after a sea-crossing many months long

Fruit from the desert
Date palms are native to Africa and the Middle East, and grow in hanging clusters, each with up to 1,500 dates.

Cocoa and chocolate
The Aztecs were the first to make chocolate from the seeds inside cocoa pods.

The world's biggest seed
Grown only in the Seychelles islands, the coco-de-mer's enormous nut weighs up to 45 lb (20 kg), making it the largest seed of any plant.

Hard seed case

Fibers surrounding seeds

Natural fibers
Before artificial fibers were invented, the kapok tree's fibers were used for stuffing mattresses and furniture.

Cones

Conifers take a long time to produce their seeds, which, as they develop, are protected by a hard cone. In trees like pines, the cone falls off intact some time after the seeds have been shed. In others, such as cedars, the cone falls apart on the tree.

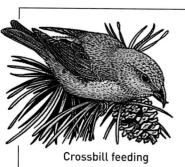

Crossbill feeding

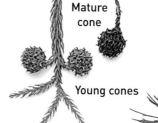

Mature cone

Young cones

Tufted cones
The cones of the Japanese cedar are ball-shaped and each scale has a feather-like tuft.

Young cones

Mature cone

Age differences
When the larch's leaves fall, greenish young cones are visible near the tips of the branches.

Young Douglas fir cones

Cones become hard and brown when mature

Mature cone

The "fake" fir
True firs have cones that fall apart on the tree. The unrelated Douglas fir has cones that fall to the ground intact.

Small cones
Unlike the cones of true cedars, the Western red cedar, a species of thuja (p. 31), has clusters of tiny cones among its leaves.

Smooth Spruce
Spruce cones are smooth and slightly flexible, unlike hard pinecones.

Young cones on branch

A giant's cones
The wellingtonia, or giant sequoia, has small round cones that take two years to ripen.

Disintegrating cone

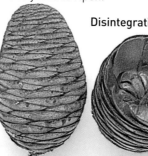

Scale with seeds

On show
Cedar cones can take three years to grow, and a number of years to disintegrate.

Mature cones

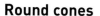

Round cones
Cypress cones are small and rounded, and often grow in clusters. When the cones are young, as this Lawson cypress shows, they are blue-green and tightly closed.

Opening up
Cypress cones have 6–12 disklike scales that part from each other as it matures, like this Monterey cypress cone.

Egg-shaped cones
The cones of true cedars are smooth and egg-shaped. They consist of a spiral stack of scales, each of which has two seeds attached to it.

Inside a pinecone

Shell surrounding seed kernel

Young cone

Scale

Mature cone

It takes up to three years for the female pine "flower" to develop from a soft, pea-sized cone into the familiar seed-bearing cone. Pine seeds develop in pairs, with two seeds being attached to each scale in the cone. In the stone pine, whose cone is shown here sliced in half, the seeds are large and have a tough shell. These seeds are the pine kernels that are used in cooking.

Young green cones

Scotch pine seeds

Mature cone

Native pine

The Scotch pine has small pointed cones. It is one of just three conifers native to Britain, alongside the yew and juniper.

Scales open in dry weather

Scales begin to close with moist air

Scales close completely in wet weather

White tips

Weymouth, or white pine, have cylindrical cones that look like spruce cones. The white marks at the tips of the scales is resin that oozes from the young cone.

A change in weather?

Pinecones can be used to forecast the weather. Cones release their seeds in dry weather; when it is damp, the scales close up to keep the seeds dry.

Paired cones of cluster pine

Sugar pine seeds have wings up to 4 cm (1.5 in) long

Cones in clusters

Cones develop from female "flowers" that grow in groups on developing shoots. Many pines have cones that develop in pairs.

Old cone that has shed most of its seeds

Californian giant

Found in the mountains of the western United States, the sugar pine has some of the largest cones of any conifer. The cones are usually about 15 in (40 cm) long, but in some specimens they can reach lengths of up to 2 ft (65 cm). A single cone can weigh as much as a pound (500 g).

Falling leaves

Leaves get their color from the green pigment they contain called chlorophyll, which harnesses the energy in sunlight. Plants often have "accessory" pigments as well that absorb light of different wavelengths, and pass on the energy to the chlorophyll. Before a deciduous tree sheds its leaves, the balance of these pigments changes, and the result is often a brilliant burst of color.

Climatic variation
Cherry leaves turn red or yellow, depending on both tree and climate.

Bred for color
Some trees are grown especially for their autumn colors. With the exquisite Japanese maples, some plant breeders have attempted to improve on nature by accentuating this feature.

Garden glory
Persian ironwood has some of the richest autumn colors of all trees. The reds, oranges, and yellows in its leaves are created by two "accessory" pigments, carotenoid and anthocyanin. Carotenoids also provide the color of many other vegetables, fruits, and flowers.

American fall
Oaks and sugar maples make up most of the colors of a New England autumn.

Yellow color produced by a carotenoid pigment

Designed for disposal
Annually, a deciduous tree, like a horse chestnut, invests a lot of energy in producing new leaves and then throwing them away. Unlike the evergreen conifers, deciduous trees do not need resins or a thick coating of wax to defend their leaves.

Colorful relatives
The more sugars a leaf contains, the brighter its autumnal colors are likely to be. The sycamore, a European maple, has fairly bright colors, but they cannot rival the brilliance of American maples.

Why leaves fall
During autumn, cork grows across the leaf stalk, eventually causing the death of the leaf.

Next year's bud
Leaf stalk
Corky layer

Pigment destruction
Working inward from the leaf's edge, this snake-bark maple shows the destruction of chlorophyll.

Transatlantic color spectrum
Most European oaks turn a dull brown in autumn, while in North America the leaves of some red oaks turn bright crimson.

Area without chlorophyll
Area with chlorophyll

Holding on
Dead leaves are not always shed immediately; young beeches keep many of their leaves until the next spring.

Internal destruction
In this hickory leaflet, the chlorophyll is being destroyed inward from the leaf edge, and outward from the leaf's midrib.

Waste removal
As well as reabsorbing minerals from its leaves, a tree also deposits waste products in them before they fall. This produces brownish colors, as in this tulip tree leaf.

Changing color
As a leaf dies, the carotenoids turn from yellow to orange to red, while scarlet anthocyanins are produced from sugars in the leaf.

The death of a tree

From the moment they germinate, trees live side by side with the organisms that will eventually kill them. Insects create small wounds in their wood, ivy scrambles up their trunks, and deadly fungal spores settles on their branches. The tree battles to survive for several years, but as less and less living wood remains, it eventually dies.

Petrified wood
Buried in a water-logged area or in peat, a tree may become petrified wood, as minerals preserve its shape.

Deer feed on sapling bark, reducing a tree's sap

Competing for light
Ivy weakens trees by reducing the light supply. As ivy climbs up, rootlets become attached to the trunk and branches.

Thick shiny leaves reduce water loss

Double trunks
The left of these two trunks is actually the stem of an old ivy plant.

A living carpet
Once wood rots, it soaks up water like a sponge, making it a perfect surface for moisture-loving plants to grow on. This dead log is covered by ferns and mosses.

Dust to dust
When wood decays, the minerals that it contains find their way back into the soil to be taken up by living trees.

Adult male stag beetle

Stag beetle larva

Rotting away
Once wood has died, fungi can attack. This branch shows the result of five years' decay on a woodland floor.

Woodlice

Feeding on wood
The larva of the stag beetle feeds on decaying wood. Woodlice feed mainly on dead plant matter and fungi.

Evergreen fronds of polypody fern

Toadstools
in dead wood

The hidden life of fungi
Toadstools are produced by certain fungi
and only appear when the fungi needs to
produce spores. The strands through
which fungi feed are hidden in the wood.

In at the kill
Many woodland fungi thrive on
the remains of a tree's death.
These toadstools are sprouting
from a decaying stump.

Creeping death
Honey fungus is deadly to
a tree. It spreads by spores
and by thick strands that grow
between the bark and wood.

Hanging down
Most toadstools
produce spores
on gills that hang
down from its cap.

Wood

Bracket fungus
Bracket fungus grows on living and dead wood. Although slow-
growing, they probably kill more trees than any other fungi. Unlike
most gilled toadstools, the brackets are hard and survive for years.

*Underside
of bracket
showing
spore-
producing
pores*

Harmless
guests
Parasites live on
nutrients "stolen"
from their tree host.
Epiphytes, like these
tropical bromeliads,
use a tree as a perch
and do it no harm.

Inside attack
The larvae of longhorn
beetles damage trees
by chewing through
the living wood.

Moss

Life among the leaves

Most animals that live on trees are invertebrates, or animals without backbones. Every tree is home to many microscopic nematode worms and to thousands or even millions of insects. To combat this drain on their resources, many trees produce a second flush of leaves in midsummer. This makes up for the losses that they suffer in spring.

Feasting on leaves
Insect larvae eat many leaves. Some, like these beetle larvae, feed on the cells between leaf veins.

Adult gall wasp

Gall falls from leaf in late summer; larva develops in leaf litter

Leaf galls
Button-shaped oak spangle galls each contain a wasp larva; bean galls on willow leaves are caused by the larva of a sawfly.

Oak marble gall

Oak apple gall

Spangle galls on oak leaf

Bean galls on willow leaves

Galls and growths
Galls are created when a tree reacts to the presence of an intruder—often the larva of a wasp. The larva lives and feeds within the gall's protective layer.

Leaf insects
These tropical insects are well camouflaged to look like the leaves they live among.

Treetop predator
The pine marten lives in the treetops. This mammal feeds at night on birds, eggs, insects, and fruit.

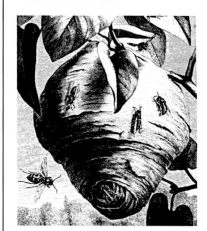

Wasp nest hanging from tree

Paper case

Entrance to nest

The paper nest
In spring, a queen wasp begins nest building. She chews wood fibers and mixes them with saliva, shaping it into layers of paper that she hangs from a branch or hole in a tree. After her first eggs hatch, the young wasps carry on nest building, and collecting food for the queen.

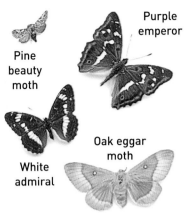
Pine beauty moth

Purple emperor

White admiral

Oak eggar moth

Butterflies and moths

The caterpillars of woodland butterflies and moths feed on the leaves of trees or ground plants. Most are harmless, but the pine beauty moth can be a pest.

Winter quarters

Every autumn, monarch butterflies migrate southward to Mexico, where they spend the winter crowded together on pine tree trunks.

Fungus attack

Tar spot fungus has attacked these maple leaves; a sign the tree grew in unpolluted air.

Infected patches turn black and expand

More and more patches of fungus appear during the summer; over half the leaf may be covered by the time it falls in autumn

Acorns attacked by weevils

Weevil

Eating seeds

Animals and insects consume seeds and nuts on the tree and ground. Weevils eat seeds by boring holes in acorns with their long "snouts."

Hazelnuts eaten by voles

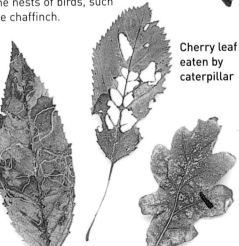

Home among the branches

The tangled lower branches of small trees provide cover for the nests of birds, such as the chaffinch.

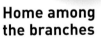
Chaffinch

Cherry leaf eaten by caterpillar

Insect pupa attached to oak leaf

Cherry leaf mined by micromoth caterpillar

Insect onslaught

The caterpillars of micromoths feed between a leaf's upper and lower surface.

Leaf-eating mammals

The only large mammals to live and feed on trees are in the tropics. Leaves here are hard to digest, so these animals spend a long time eating.

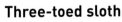

Three-toed sloth

This South American animal spends its whole life hanging upside down.

Koala

Koalas live almost entirely on eucalyptus leaves (p. 13).

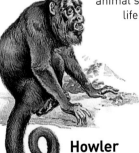

Howler monkey

South American howler monkeys use their tails to climb through the treetops in search of leaves.

A plane drops water on flames to extinguish a wildfire

Wildfires

Wildfires pose a serious threat to plants, animals, humans, and property. With ground temperatures reaching more than 1,800°F (1,000°C), wildfires affect most continents, especially places with hot and dry seasons, such as Australia. Despite the dangers, wildfires benefit some forests. For example, they help return nutrients to the soil by burning dead or decaying matter.

What fuels it?
Many wildfires are set off by lightning or dry weather. They can also be caused by human carelessness, such as a dropped match. Winds can pick up and carry sparks or a small piece of glowing wood, starting new fires.

Dousing the flames
There are different methods for containing wildfires. These include the construction of tall lookout posts from which a person can spot a fire and alert firefighters. Natural or man-made gaps in the vegetation can break the fire's path. Planes can also spray retardants to control the flames.

Charred trees after a wildfire

Fresh start
Some wildfires give a new lease on life to forests, as they restore nutrients in the soil by burning waste matter. They also rid the forest of diseased plants, harmful insects, and pests. In addition, as thick canopies and brushy undergrowth get burned away, sunlight is able to reach plants on the usually dark forest floor, helping seedlings to grow.

Climber on a giant sequoia tree

Survival tactics
Some trees and plant species have fireproof qualities and can survive the hottest wildfires. Fully grown giant sequoias, for example, have fibrous, fire-resistant bark that can grow up to 20 in (50 cm) thick, which allows them to withstand intense fires.

Resin, which glues shut the cone, melts during a wildfire

Lodgepole pinecones

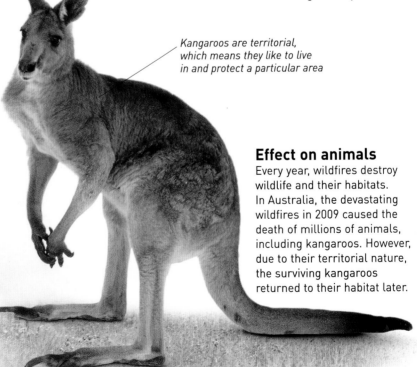

Kangaroos are territorial, which means they like to live in and protect a particular area

Giving life to trees
Wildfires help certain trees continue their species, often by reducing competition. In some cases, these fires help trees germinate. For example, the intense heat of a wildfire causes the thick and hard cones of the lodgepole pine to open and release its seeds.

Effect on animals
Every year, wildfires destroy wildlife and their habitats. In Australia, the devastating wildfires in 2009 caused the death of millions of animals, including kangaroos. However, due to their territorial nature, the surviving kangaroos returned to their habitat later.

Pollution and disease

Trees need clean air if they are to grow and work efficiently. Across many parts of the world, fumes from cars, factories, and power stations pollute the air. These gases reach high into the atmosphere and mix with water and other chemicals to form "acid rain" that is responsible for the decline of many forests.

Dying tree
It is hard to know what is causing this yew tree to die. Drought and severe frost may be partly to blame, or a disease caused by a virus. Acid rain makes the tree vulnerable to damage, and so is at least indirectly responsible for its death.

A future in doubt
Acid rain may now threaten the lives of centuries-old churchyard yew trees.

Discoloration of leaves—this may be a direct effect of acid rain, which enables ozone in the atmosphere to disrupt the chemistry of the leaves

Deep green color shows the leaf is full of chlorophyll, the substance essential for harnessing the Sun's energy

Long shoots indicate healthy growth

Healthy leaves survive well on each twig and along the branches

Healthy tree
The damage caused by air pollution strikes coniferous and broadleaved trees. It is easiest to see in conifers because their scales and needles stay on the tree for years, and visual signs of sickness can build up.

City dweller
The London plane fares well in polluted urban air. Whereas most city trees become blackened with grime, it sheds its outermost layers, revealing young bark underneath.

Dieback of leading shoots

The "tinsel effect"— a sign of sickness in which the area behind the tip of each twig loses its leaves

Tree sickness

Certain diseases are extremely harmful. For example, chalara dieback of ash is a disease that leads to leaf loss and usually kills the tree. Similarly, chestnut blight has killed about 3.8 billion trees in the past 20 years in Europe and North America alone.

Chestnut blight lesions on American chestnut tree bark

Dark-colored moths

After the Industrial Revolution, the peppered moth evolved to become darker: this color provided it with better camouflage against tree trunks blackened by soot.

A dying forest

Acid rain damage was first noticed in the early 1970s, largely through its disastrous effect on the wildlife of Scandinavian lakes. Since then it has hit coniferous forests throughout Europe, and is an increasing problem in North America.

Coniferous trees affected by acid rain

Pesky pests

Insect borers, such as bark beetles, tunnel into the shoots, branches, trunks, or roots of woody plants, and can lay eggs on or in the bark. On hatching, the young beetles chew their way into the plant tissue, which carries essential nutrients.

How acid rain forms

Acid rain is produced largely by two gases—sulphur oxide and nitrogen oxide—released by factories, power stations, and cars. When the gases mix with water in the atmosphere, they form tiny acid droplets. These fall as acid rain, which attacks plant leaves and leaches nutrients from the soil. The most effective way to prevent acid rain is by reducing the emission of sulphur and nitrogen oxides.

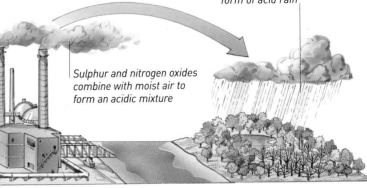

The acidic mixture falls on Earth in the form of acid rain

Sulphur and nitrogen oxides combine with moist air to form an acidic mixture

From tree to timber

Today, machines do almost all the work of turning trees into timber. Power saws make short work of the thickest trunks, and then giant, hydraulically operated jaws handle them on their way to the sawmill. Once at the mill, a log is loaded onto a sliding cradle and is sliced into boards. Two simple methods of cutting are shown here, but there are many other methods, all designed to extract the maximum amount of good quality wood from a log. Nothing is wasted: whatever remains will end up as chipboard or pulp.

The spring log run
Traditionally, water power was used to get logs to the sawmill. Breaking up log jams was a skilled business, but log runs, like the one shown here, damaged the water and river banks. Today, they are rarely seen.

Forest sawmill
As settlers moved farther westward in North America, sawmills were set up to provide timber for their houses, barns, and wagons.

"Through and through" sawing
This is the simplest way of sawing a log. However, the way the cuts are made through the grain means that the boards are liable to warp, so it is rarely used with expensive timber.

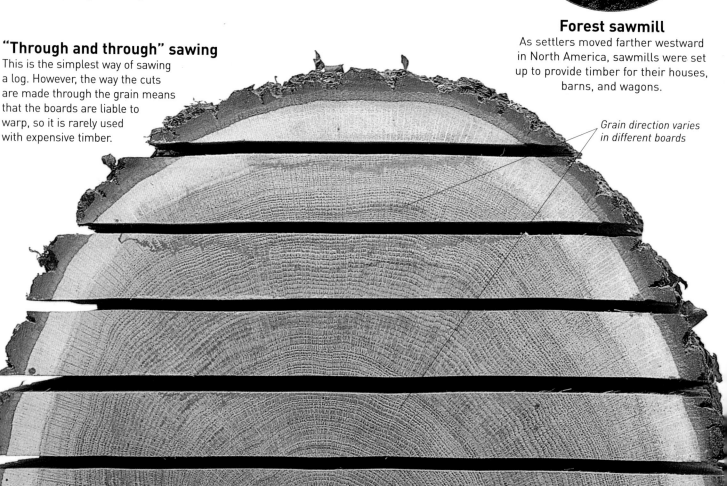

Grain direction varies in different boards

56

Quarter sawing
This method is wasteful, but it produces boards that have a decorative grain and which retain their shape well.

Woodworking
Logs are sawn when still full of sap. Before it can be used, the timber must first be left to dry, which can take more than a year. The timber is then sawn again into workable lengths. This engraving of a cabinetmaker's shop shows the final stages in its journey: planing, carving, glueing, and joining.

Making veneers
A veneer is a thin layer of wood. Veneers of expensive hardwoods are used for decoration and to cover cheaper timber. Veneers are traditionally cut in three ways: slicing, sawing, and peeling.

Slicing
This is used with woods such as walnut and maple to produce decorative grain patterns.

Radial boards all run at right angles to the growth rings

These segments are cut into smaller-sized boards

Sawing
Cutting veneers with a circular saw is only done on woods that are particularly hard.

Peeling
Many veneers are cut by rotating each log against a stationary blade to produce a continuous sheet of wood.

Working with wood

People who work with wood traditionally divide it into two types: "hardwood," which comes from broadleaved trees, and "softwood," which comes from conifers. Sometimes these two words can be misleading. Yew, for example, is a softwood, but it is actually as hard as oak. Balsa, on the other hand, is a hardwood, even though it is soft and lightweight.

Melanesian carving

Planed yew

Close grain produced by slow growth

Unplaned yew

Dense knots typical of yew wood

Planed cherry wood

Light pinkish coloring typical of freshly cut cherry wood

Knot

Changing color
Many woods, such as cherry wood, change color when exposed to the air. Over time, this wood grows darker, until—as in old pieces of furniture—it becomes a deep red.

The bowmaker's wood
Yew grows very slowly, and this gives the wood great weight and strength. Traditionally used to make longbows, today wood from yew trunks is often used as a decorative veneer.

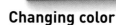

The merry maypole
Dancing around a wooden pole is an old custom. Various woods have been used to make the pole.

The gunsmith's wood
Rich-colored walnut is traditionally used to make the stocks of guns. This wood can be worked into a comfortable shape, and can also stand the sharp jolt of a gun being fired without splitting.

The versatile larch
Wherever a cheap, tough wood is needed, larch is often the ideal choice. It can be used to make furniture and boats; much of the rest can be used to make paper.

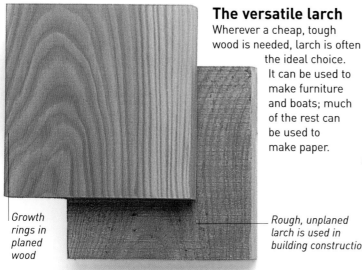

Growth rings in planed wood

Rough, unplaned larch is used in building construction

Planed walnut

Unpolished walnut

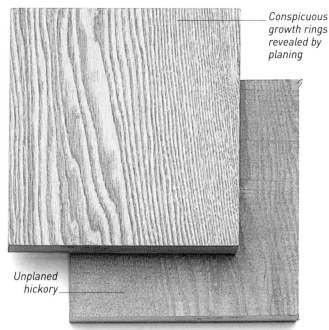

Conspicuous growth rings revealed by planing

Unplaned hickory

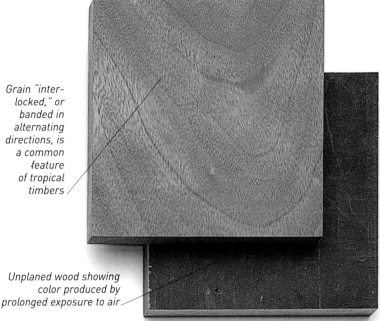

Grain "inter-locked," or banded in alternating directions, is a common feature of tropical timbers

Unplaned wood showing color produced by prolonged exposure to air

Nature's shock absorber

Ash wood is ideal for the handles of axes and spades. In Europe, it was always the first choice for the handles of tools, until hickory—an even better shock absorber than ash—started to be exported from North America.

Tropical treasure

Mahogany became highly prized after Spanish sailors brought back Caribbean mahogany for King Philip II in the 16th century. Since then, the world's best hardwood forests have diminished in size.

Skilled woodworker

This engraving shows a turner, a craftsman who makes wooden objects using a lathe. The craft dates back to the ancient Egyptians, who made many high-quality chair legs and stools.

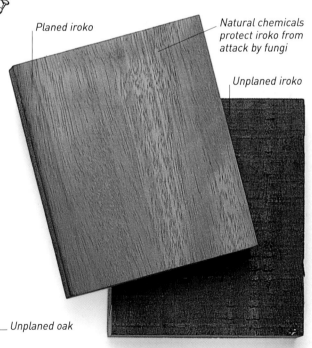

Planed iroko

Natural chemicals protect iroko from attack by fungi

Unplaned iroko

Planed oak

Sap-conducting pores appear as tiny streaks in the grain of oak

Unplaned oak

Withstanding the elements

Some woods are more hardy that others. A garden bench made of beech would collapse within a few years, while one made of the tropical timber iroko could last for decades.

Heart of oak

Once used in buildings, oak is one of the world's strongest timbers. To support the dome of St. Paul's Cathedral in London, for example, Sir Christopher Wren ordered oak beams nearly 50 ft (15 m) long.

Tree care and management

Special techniques have been used to "manage" trees since prehistoric times. These include coppicing (regularly cutting trees at ground level), pollarding (lopping the tops of trees), and the selective felling of trees. Tree planting probably began with species such as the date palm and olive (pp. 39 and 43), which were grown for their fruit. Today, pruning and grafting help to shape a tree, prevent disease, and increase fruit yields.

Grafting
By grafting shoots from one tree on to the branches or trunk of another it is possible to introduce good characteristics, such as healthy fruit or a strong trunk.

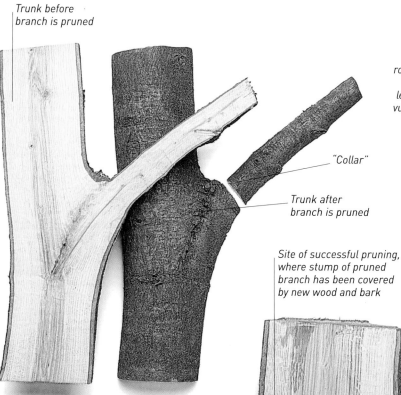

Trunk before branch is pruned

"Collar"

Trunk after branch is pruned

Site of successful pruning, where stump of pruned branch has been covered by new wood and bark

Hole left by wood rotting after branch has fallen away, leaving damp wood vulnerable to attack by fungi

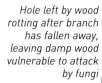

Pruning
This technique is mainly used on fruit trees or on trees with large, unsafe branches. When pruning a branch, a tree surgeon will first cut through the branch about 18 in (50 cm) from the trunk. Then a cut is made, either a "flush cut" close to the trunk, or a cut at the "collar," which is the point at which the branch begins to widen just before meeting the trunk. The exposed wood is then treated with a waterproofing agent and a fungicide. As the tree grows, the wood will become covered with a layer of living wood and protective bark.

Water traps
Pools of water can be found where branches have broken off, which can lead to wood decay. Likewise, where branches meet, water may collect and provoke fungal attack. This problem can be resolved by cutting a drainage channel through the wood, or by permanently inserting a metal tube that drains off the water.

Coppicing and pollarding

Coppiced trees are regularly cut at ground level to produce straight stems. Pollarded trees regularly have their tops cut off, which create long branches from shoots too high to be damaged by cattle and deer.

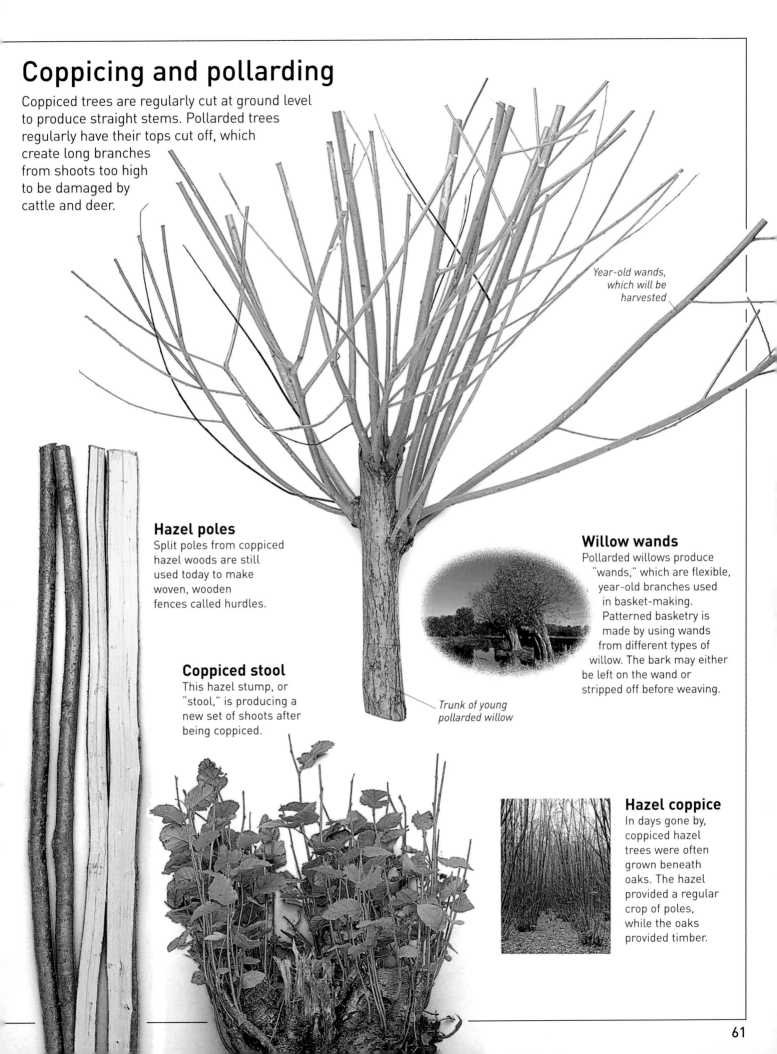

Year-old wands, which will be harvested

Hazel poles
Split poles from coppiced hazel woods are still used today to make woven, wooden fences called hurdles.

Willow wands
Pollarded willows produce "wands," which are flexible, year-old branches used in basket-making. Patterned basketry is made by using wands from different types of willow. The bark may either be left on the wand or stripped off before weaving.

Coppiced stool
This hazel stump, or "stool," is producing a new set of shoots after being coppiced.

Trunk of young pollarded willow

Hazel coppice
In days gone by, coppiced hazel trees were often grown beneath oaks. The hazel provided a regular crop of poles, while the oaks provided timber.

Deforestation and conservation

Farming and logging have led to the depletion of forests, which affects the lives of plants, trees, and animals. Conservation is the process of protecting trees, and various organizations are now working toward forest conservation to preserve their wildlife and habitats.

Saving trees
The two main ways of protecting forests are reforestation and afforestation. Reforestation is the reestablishment of forest cover by planting trees. Afforestation is the building of a new forest or a cluster of trees in an area where there was previously none. Many countries are now involved in planting forests, including China.

Coastal deforestation
Deforestation, or clearing an area of trees in a forest, has wiped out many of the world's forests. Loss of trees in such great numbers can harm the environment, lead to the extinction of many species of plants and animals, and increase soil erosion. Since trees are a natural barrier against waves, cutting down trees along coasts can lead to massive soil erosion and flooding as well.

Cutting them down

Trees are cut down—or logged—for many reasons. These include clearing land for cattle, providing timber to produce paper or furniture, and to make space for growing cities.

Log loader at a conifer log mill

Useful products

Trees are a source of many "non-timber forest products," from food to cosmetic gels. However, scientists fear that if humans clear forests at the present rate, there will not be enough trees left from which people can get essential products, including medicine.

Aloe vera gel

Aloe vera leaves

Cloves

Clove oil

Eucalyptus oil

Eucalyptus leaves

Endangered animals

Animals are under threat due to deforestation. The silky sifaka lemurs, which live in the forests of Madagascar, are one of the top 25 most endangered primates on Earth because their habitat is at risk. South America's Atlantic Forest is home to more than 24 critically endangered vertebrate species that are struggling to survive as humans continue to destroy their home.

Silky sifaka lemur

Climate change

Greenhouse gases, such as carbon dioxide, from factories and cars are warming up the atmosphere. Forests play an important role, as trees absorb greenhouse gases and help to regulate temperature.

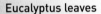

Did you know?

AMAZING FACTS

Oak tree

Acorn and oak leaves

A mature oak tree grows about 250,000 leaves every year. In a good year it also produces about 50,000 acorns.

The leaves of the African raffia palm can be as long as 83 ft (25 m).

The titan arum of the Indonesian rain forest is the world's largest flower, standing up to 10 ft (3 m) tall and 5 ft (1.5 m) wide. However, its scent is the smell of rotten flesh.

The needles on one of the oldest trees, the bristlecone pine tree, can live for 20 to 30 years.

An ancient yew tree in France has a girth of over 33 ft (10 m). In the 18th century, a French barber used the tree's hollow trunk as his workplace.

About 30 million Christmas trees are sold each year in the USA alone.

When flood deposits raise the level of the ground, most trees die because their root systems are smothered. But coastal redwood trees are able to grow a new root system. Some coastal redwoods have survived a rise in ground level of up to 30 ft (9 m). Redwoods can also survive for a long time in a flood.

The chapel-oak at Allouville in Bellefosse, France, is an amazing ancient oak tree that has two chapels inside its hollow trunk. The first chapel was established in 1669, and, later, a second chapel was built above it, together with a wooden entrance stairway. The oak is not as healthy as it once was, but it is still an impressive sight.

The giant lime tree in Heede, Germany, is the biggest tree in Germany, and probably the biggest lime tree in Europe. Its enormous trunk has a girth of 56.7 ft (17.3 m).

About 4 million trees are planted in the USA every day.

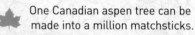

Matches

Aspen trees

One Canadian aspen tree can be made into a million matchsticks.

A fully grown birch tree can produce a million seeds in one year.

The talipot palm produces a flower spike that is an amazing 33 ft (10 m) high. The palm flowers only once before it dies.

The baobab tree has soft, spongy wood that stores water absorbed by the roots. Elephants sometimes rip the tree open with their tusks to drink when water is scarce.

People in England have less woodland to enjoy than almost any other European country. Only about 10 percent of England's landscape is covered in trees, whereas in Europe the average is about 30 percent.

The ancient Mayans made chewing gum from the sap of the spruce tree, sapodilla, which is native to Central America.

The bark of a giant sequoia tree can be up to 2 ft (0.7 m) thick. When exposed to fire, the giant sequoia's bark chars to form a heat shield, protecting the tree.

The Major Oak in Sherwood Forest Country Park, England, weighs 25.3 tons (23 metric tons), has a girth of 33 ft (10 m), and a spread of 92 ft (28 m). It is the biggest oak tree in Britain.

The Major Oak, Sherwood Forest Country Park, England

QUESTIONS AND ANSWERS

The tree line in the Alps

Q What information can you get from looking at tree rings?

A Tree rings provide information about the climate in the past. They can show the effects of specific events, such as volcanic eruptions. Dendrochronology is the science of dating trees from their rings.

Q Do all tree roots grow underground?

A Most do, but in the banyan tree, roots also grow down from branches.

Each ring represents a period of growth

A slice of tree trunk, showing tree rings

Q What is the tree line?

A The height above sea-level at which trees cannot grow is called the tree line. The tree line in the Alps in Europe is between 6,560 ft (2,000 m) and 8,200 ft (2,500 m), but in northern Scandinavia, it can be as low as 820 ft (250 m).

Q How much timber do you need to make paper?

A It takes approximately 2.2 tons (2 metric tons) of timber to make 1.1 ton (1 metric ton) of paper.

Pillar roots on a banyan tree

Q When is the best time of year to transplant a tree?

A In the summer time, a tree is busy making food and growing. In the autumn and winter, the tree is resting, and if you need to move a tree, this is the best time to do it.

Q Where does resin come from?

A Resin is a sticky liquid that is produced by certain pine trees. It is used to make turpentine.

Inside a paper-making factory

Q Why are tree fruits often red?

A Tree fruits are dispersed by animals. Many berries turn red when their seeds are ripe, since red is a preferred food color of birds.

Q How do mangroves cope with all the salty water they absorb?

A Black mangrove trees get rid of a lot of the salt through their leaves, which can be covered in salt crystals.

Record Breakers

General Sherman in California, USA

THE WORLD'S LARGEST TREE
A giant sequoia known as "General Sherman" is the largest tree in the world. It stands at 275 ft (83.8 m) and its volume is 52,513 cubic ft (1,487 cubic m).

THE TALLEST TREE IN THE WORLD
Hyperion, a coastal redwood in California, USA, is the tallest tree at 379 ft (115.6 m).

THE WORLD'S OLDEST TREE
A spruce tree in Sweden is estimated to be almost 10,000 years, making it the oldest.

THE HIGHEST HEDGE IN THE WORLD
Planted in 1745, the highest hedge is in Scotland and is 118 ft (36 m) tall.

BRITAIN'S OLDEST TREE
The Fortingall Yew in Tayside, Scotland, is about 3,000 years old, and Britain's oldest.

Identifying trees

The first stage in identifying a tree is to figure out whether it is a conifer or a broadleaf. This section outlines the main differences between them and provides common examples from each group.

CONIFERS

If a tree is bearing cones, it is a conifer. The fruit of most conifers is a cone with woody scales, although in some, such as the juniper, the scales are fleshy so that the fruit appears more like a berry. Most conifers are evergreen (keep their leaves in winter), but a few are deciduous (lose their leaves in autumn). Conifer leaves are usually small, needle- or scalelike, and often smell sweet.

The cones turn brown

The cones have upright scales

The leaves are soft

The Italian cypress is an evergreen; its scalelike leaves are dark green.

The needles grow in pairs

The stone pine tree is an evergreen, has long, needlelike leaves, and a round, brown cone.

The leaves grow in whorls

The European larch has needlelike leaves, but is deciduous. The green leaves turn yellow in autumn.

The fruit turns red as it expands

The cone has pointed scales

The common yew bears a berrylike "fruit;" its evergreen leaves are on the sides of the shoot.

The monkey puzzle is an evergreen with prickly, toothlike leaves all around the shoot.

BROADLEAVED TREES

All broadleaved trees bear flowers, and produce their seeds inside fruits, not inside cones. The fruits of broadleaved trees are varied—rough, smooth, or spiny; edible or inedible; woody or fleshy; many different colors—depending on the way in which the seeds are dispersed. Most broadleaved trees have broad, flat leaves. Many are deciduous, but some are evergreen.

The apple tree is deciduous. Its pink flowers are conspicuous and its fruit is fleshy.

The leaf has rounded lobes

The sessile oak tree is deciduous. Its leaves are simple, which means that they are undivided. The flowers are green and inconspicuous. The fruit is an acorn, which is a type of nut.

The horse chestnut tree is deciduous. Each leaf is made up of five sharply toothed leaflets. Its white, pink, or red flowers are very conspicuous. Its fruit, the "conker," is a type of nut.

The honey locust tree has divided leaves. It is deciduous. Its yellow-green flowers are conspicuous, and the fruit is a long, brown hanging pod.

The bright red berries are large and fleshy

The holly tree is an evergreen with simple leaves, many of which are spiny. It has small, white flowers and bright, red berries.

The silver gum eucalyptus is an evergreen with small, blue-gray leaves and white flowers.

PALMS

Palms are broadleaved trees, but they have many special features. Their trunks hardly ever branch, and they do not have true bark. Palm leaves are often shaped like giant fans, and can last for many years. Palm flowers are often small and green, but the fruit can be large. Most palms need a warm climate and grow in the tropics.

The chusan palm has fan-shaped leaves up to 4 ft (120 cm) across. It has yellow flowers and its fruit is a blue-black berry. It copes well in cold weather.

The coconut palm is found in the warm tropics. It needs a lot of water. It has giant, featherlike leaves and its fruit is the coconut.

Find out more

There are many ways of finding out more about trees. You could go on a visit to an arboretum, and see how many different trees you can identify. You could take care of wooded areas in your region by joining your local woodland group. Or you could support a charity that reestablishes woodland in areas where it has been lost.

Take care of your local woodland

Join a local nature conservancy group and look after woods in your area to ensure that they remain healthy and provide a good habitat for the local wildlife. Old trees may need pollarding, or even felling, and young trees need planting and ongoing care.

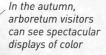

In the autumn, arboretum visitors can see spectacular displays of color

Visit an arboretum

An arboretum is a garden that focuses on the cultivation of trees and shrubs. They are often grouped according to the climate in which they naturally grow. It is a great place to experience trees from many different parts of the world. Many arboreta were started in the 19th century, so they now contain large, mature trees.

Explore Eden's biomes

Visit the giant biomes at the Eden Project in Cornwall, England, to see trees and other plants from the warm temperate regions of the world. It is an exciting place to visit, and is also a place that aims to increase awareness of the effect people have on their environment.

Support a charity

Find out more about charities, and support them, either with your time or by fundraising. The Nature Conservancy's Plant a Billion Trees campaign is working to reforest areas all over the world. MillionTreesNYC helps to engage communities in New York City in tree-planting events.

Newspapers

Cardboard

How much wood do you use?

For many countries, timber is a major import. Britain, for example, produces only one-tenth of the wood it needs. See if you can cut down on how much wood you use.

Pencil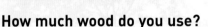

Paper

Native trees

A good way of increasing your knowledge about trees is to start a collection. By collecting the leaves, making bark rubbings, and sketching the fruits and the tree shapes, you will learn to identify a number of trees. As you do so, work out which trees are from your country, and which are not.

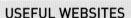

USEFUL WEBSITES

- National Forest Foundation aims to improve people's appreciation and knowledge of trees and forests. For information, go to
  www.nationalforests.org
- To find out about the forest conservation efforts of The Nature Conservancy, visit
  www.nature.org
- For details on how to take care of trees, see
  www.arborday.org/trees/tips/
- For details on how to identify trees, visit
  www.arborday.org/trees/whattree/
- For information on the Wildlife Conservation Society, go to
  www.wcs.org
- To learn about the U.S. Forest Service, which is responsible for the protection of America's forests and woodlands, see
  www.fs.fed.us
- For information on native North American trees, go to
  www.na.fs.fed.us/spfo/pubs/silvics_ manual/table_of_contents.htm

PLACES TO VISIT

THE UNITED STATES BOTANIC GARDENS, WASHINGTON, D.C.
- Explore the Jungle room and the rest of the extensive gardens.

THE UNITED STATES NATIONAL ARBORETUM, WASHINGTON, D.C.
- This 446-acre arboretum is located right in Washington, D.C.

NEW YORK BOTANICAL GARDEN, NEW YORK, NEW YORK
- Visit America's leading urban garden. Check out the 50 acres of old-growth forest, which is a remnant of the woodland that used to cover all of New York City.

REDWOOD NATIONAL AND STATE PARKS, NORTHERN CALIFORNIA
- These four parks are home to the mighty California Redwood, which is one of the tallest and oldest living trees on Earth.

CHICAGO BOTANIC GARDEN, GLENCOE, ILLINOIS
- There is plenty to see at this botanic garden, from the Bonsai Collection to the Dwarf Conifer Garden, and much more.

FAIRCHILD TROPICAL BOTANIC GARDEN, CORAL GABLES, FLORIDA
- This impressive botanic garden has a wonderful palm collection, or palmetum. The Montgomery Palmetum is 13 acres and displays 1000 palms.

THE HOLDEN ARBORETUM, KIRTLAND, OHIO
- The Holden Aboretum is one of the largest arboreta in the United States. There are guided tours and a range of special events.

The visitor's center at the Arboretum National des Barres, France

Glossary

ANTHER The part of a stamen that produces pollen.

BARK A "skin" of hard, dead tissue that protects the living inner parts of the tree. The bark stretches as the trunk or branch grows. Most trees replace their bark from time to time.

BLOSSOM The flowers of a tree, especially one that produces edible fruit.

BRACT The leaflike structure just below a flower.

BRANCH A secondary woody stem coming from the trunk of a tree.

BROADLEAVED Bearing broad, flat leaves.

BUD The swelling on a plant made up of overlapping, immature leaves or petals. Most buds are protected by a layer of thick scales.

CAMBIUM A thin layer of cells that covers the whole of a tree, just underneath its bark. When its cells multiply—usually in spring and summer—the tree's trunk, branches, and roots get longer and fatter.

CANOPY High-level foliage in a forest, formed by the crowns of the trees.

CATKIN A cluster of bracts and tiny flowers, usually male. Catkins release millions of pollen grains in spring or early summer.

CELLULOSE A substance that forms a major part of the cell walls of trees and many other plants. Cellulose strengthens the stems, roots, and leaves.

A deciduous tree

Catkins

CHLOROPHYLL The green pigment in plants that traps the energy of sunlight and uses it to make sugars through photosynthesis.

COMPOUND LEAF A leaf composed of two or more leaflets. Compound leaves grow from a single bud.

CONE The round, scaly "fruit" carried by a conifer tree. There are two types of cone. The small, soft male cones produce and release pollen, then shrivel and die. The larger female cones become woody as they get older. Their scales contain ovules that develop into seeds when fertilized by pollen.

Cone

CONIFER A cone-bearing tree with small, needle- or scalelike leaves. Most conifers are evergreen.

COPPICING Cutting back a tree at ground level so that it grows lots of straight stems, often used in fences.

CROWN The rounded, top part of a broadleaf tree.

DECIDUOUS A tree that loses its leaves in autumn.

DIOECIOUS Having male and female flowers on separate plants. Only the female plants produce seeds.

DISPERSAL The way in which a tree spreads its seeds. Birds and other animals disperse seeds by eating fruits or berries and passing the seeds in their droppings. Squirrels and other mammals hide nuts as a food store, and some of them germinate. Some seeds are dispersed by the wind, others by water.

EVERGREEN A tree that keeps its leaves in winter.

FRUIT The ripened ovary of a flowering plant, containing one or more seeds.

GERMINATION The sprouting of a seed or spore. Some seeds germinate very soon after they are shed; others survive all winter and germinate in the spring.

GIRDLE SCAR The mark on a branch showing where one season's growth ended and the next season's began.

GIRTH The circumference or distance around a tree's trunk.

GRAFTING Fixing a shoot from one tree onto the cut stem of another one.

HARDWOOD The wood of any broadleaved tree.

HARDY Plants that survive in difficult conditions, especially in winter.

HEARTWOOD The hard wood at the center of the tree that helps to support the tree.

HUMUS Dark brown, organic matter in the soil that improves its fertility.

KERNEL The edible seed within the shell of a nut or the pit of a fruit.

LATERAL BUD The bud on the side of a trunk that develops into flowers or a twig with either leaves or leaves and flowers.

LEADING BUD The bud at the tip of a branch that develops into shoots to make the branch longer.

LEAF A green, usually flat, blade attached to a tree. Leaves make food for the tree by photosynthesis.

LEAF SCAR The mark left on a branch by a fallen leaf from the previous growing season.

LEAFLET A small leaf, or part of a compound leaf.

LEAF LITTER A layer of partly decomposed leaves and twigs.

A conifer tree twig with needles and cones

LIGNIN The substance found in the cell walls of woody tissue that makes the tree hard and stiff.

LOBE A rounded section of a leaf.

MAST The fruit of forest trees.

MONOECIOUS A plant that has both male and female reproductive organs.

NATIVE A plant that originates in a particular place.

NATURALIZED A plant that has adapted successfully to a foreign environment.

NECTAR A sugary fluid produced by flowers. Nectar attracts insects such as bees and butterflies that pollinate the flower while collecting the nectar.

NEEDLES The long, narrow, stiff leaves of coniferous trees.

NUT A dry fruit containing one seed encased in a woody wall. A nut does not naturally burst open to disperse the seed.

OVARY The female part of the flower that produces the ovules.

OVULE The section of the flower that contains the egg cell. After fertilization, the ovule develops into the seed.

PALMATE A leaf with five lobes that spread out in the shape of a hand.

PARASITE A plant or animal that lives in or on another plant or animal.

PHOTOSYNTHESIS A process that uses the energy from sunlight to turn carbon dioxide and water into sugars. This fuels the plant's growth.

PIGMENT The substance that gives color to another material.

POLLARDING Cutting the top off a tree to encourage more bushy growth or to reduce the size of large trees.

POLLEN A sticky or dusty ubstance produced by a flower's anthers. Pollen contains the plant's male sex cells.

POLLINATE To transfer pollen from the anthers to the stigma of a flower. Animals, usually insects, pollinate many flowers, while others are pollinated by the wind.

PRUNING Cutting branches off a tree to improve the shape of a fruit tree, or to remove large branches that are no longer safe.

RECEPTACLE The top of the flower stalk that bears the parts of the flower. After pollination, the receptacle may swell to form the fruit.

ROOT The part of the plant that anchors it in the soil and absorbs water and minerals.

ROOT HAIRS Fine hairs near the tip of a root that soak up water and dissolved minerals.

SEEDLING The young tree that develops from a seed.

SAP Water containing dissolved minerals that is carried from the roots to the leaves in tiny pipelines in the sapwood.

SAPLING A young tree that is about 6 ft (1.8 m) tall with a trunk that is 1 to 2 in (2.5 to 5 cm) thick.

SAPWOOD The soft wood in a tree, situated just inside the cambium layer. Sapwood is made up of living cells and contains tiny pipelines that carry sap.

SEED The mature, fertilized ovule of a plant. Inside the seed case is the embryo and its food store. Some seeds are contained in fruits and berries, others in nuts, still others in pods or cones.

SEPALS The parts of a flower that protect the developing flower bud.

SIMPLE LEAF A leaf that is not divided into leaflets.

SOFTWOOD The wood of any coniferous tree, such as pine and cedar.

SPREAD The area occupied by a tree, including all its branches.

STAMEN The male, reproductive part of a flower, consisting of filaments (stalks) bearing anthers.

STIGMA The upper part of the ovary. Pollen passes through the stigma to enter the ovary.

STYLE The slender part of the ovary that bears the stigma.

Variegated leaf

TOOTHED A leaf with sharp ndentations along its edge.

TRUNK The main stem of a tree. On most conifers, the trunk grows straight to the top of the tree. On most broadleaf trees, the trunk does not reach the top, but divides into branches.

VARIEGATED A leaf that is green in parts and not in others, where hlorophyll is absent.

WOOD The hard, fibrous substance beneath the bark in trees and shrubs. Wood consists mainly of cellulose.

Leaf litter

Index

A

acacia 28
acid rain 54, 55
acorn woodpeckers 20
acorns 2, 8, 14, 20, 41, 51
Adam and Eve 38
afforestation 62
alder 32, 40, 41
algae 20
aloe vera 63
amber 23
animals 50, 53
  burrowing 19
  destruction 51
  pollination 34–37
ants, 53
apples 2, 3, 32, 35, 38, 39, 67
ash, 3, 6, 16, 22, 25, 28, 29, 41, 55, 59

B

badgers 18, 19
banyan 6, 13, 65
baobab 37, 43, 64
bark 6, 11, 22–23, 70
  damage 20
Barringtonia 42
bat pollination 37
beech 8, 9, 14, 15, 22, 25, 40, 65
  copper 26
  mast 25, 40
beetles 21, 48, 50, 55
berries 38–39
bilberry 53
birch 23–25, 41, 64
birds 20, 21, 37, 38, 39, 51
  food 39
  nests 51
  pollination 37
  seed dispersal 38
bitternut 28
blackthorn 35, 39
branches 9, 10, 16, 65, 70
brazil nuts 42
breadfruit 42
broadleaves 7–9, 12, 28, 32, 67
bromeliads 21, 49
buckeyes 29
buds 24–25, 70
butterflies 51

C

cambium 16, 17, 22, 70
catalpa 27, 37
catkins 32, 33, 40, 70
cedar 2, 30, 31, 44
  blue atlas 2, 30
  Japanese 44
  Western red 4, 44
cellulose 26, 70
chalara dieback 55
cherry 23, 26, 34, 46, 51
cherry plum 39
chestnut
  blight 55
  horse 23, 24, 29, 35, 40, 46, 67
  sweet 26, 40
chlorophyll 26, 46, 47, 54, 70
chocolate 43
Christmas conifers, 11, 31, 64
cinchona 22
cinnamon 23
climate change 63
cloves 63
coco-de-mer 43
coconut 13, 42, 43
colour 26, 30, 38, 46, 47, 58
cones 10, 11, 32, 44–45, 66, 70
conifers 7, 10–11, 18, 23, 30, 31, 32, 54–55, 66, 70
conkers 35, 40
conservation 62–63
coppicing 61, 70
cork 22, 47
cultivation 34, 35, 39, 60, 61
cycads 7
cypress 10, 18, 30, 31, 32, 44
  Italian 66
  Lawson 4, 32, 44
  Monterey 2
  sawara 30
  swamp 18, 31

D

damsons 39
Daphne 7
dates 43
decay, 48, 49, 55
deciduous 6, 8, 46, 70
deciduous conifer 18, 66
deer 48
deforestation 62–63
destruction 16
disease 50, 51, 54–55, 60
dispersal of seeds 38, 40–42, 71
dogwood 37
drip tip 12

EF

ecosystem 53, 62
elder 37, 38
embryo 14
environment 8, 16, 18
eucalyptus 12, 13, 22, 63, 67
evergreen 10, 66, 70
ferns 21, 48
filberts 40
fir 30
  Douglas 44
fire fighting 52–53
flowers 32–37
fly agaric 19
fossils 10, 23, 31
fruit 38–43, 67, 70
fungi 3, 19, 20, 48, 49, 51, 55

GH

galls 41, 50
germination 14, 15, 53, 70
giant bamboo 7
ginkgo 2, 37
Glastonbury thorn 36
grafting 60, 70
Great Green Wall of China 62
growth 16, 17
  patterns 9, 11
  rings 8, 10, 16, 17, 59, 65
hardwood 58, 70
hawthorn 36, 38
hazel 2, 3, 23, 31, 61
heartwood 16, 17
Hercules club 29
hickory 28, 33, 47, 59
holly 4, 11, 26, 67
honey locust 67
hop 28
hornbeam 32
hornbills 21
hummingbirds 37

IJK

insects 20, 48, 50–51
  pests 53, 55
  pollination 34–36
iroko 59
ivy 48
judas 26, 36
juniper 31
kangaroos 51
kapok 37, 43

katsura 26
Kentucky coffee 29
koala bears 13, 51

L

laburnum 28, 41
larch 4, 30, 31, 32, 44, 58, 66
laurel 7
leaf litter 8, 10, 70
leaves, 8, 9, 12, 14, 15, 26–31, 46–47, 50–51, 70, 71
  variegated 26
legends, 6, 7, 11, 38
lemons 39
lemurs 63
lichens 8, 21
lightning 52, 53
lignin 26, 70
lime 41, 64
logging 63

MN

mace 42
magnolia 2, 25, 26
mahogany 59
mangoes 43
mangroves 18, 65
maple 4, 8, 20, 23, 26, 27, 28, 36, 40, 46, 47, 57
  Japanese 26, 27
  Norway 20–21
  snake bark 27, 47
  sugar 46
syrup 23
maypoles 58
medlars 39
medullary rays 17
micromoths 8, 51
minerals 48
mistletoe 21, 49
monkey pots 42
monkey puzzle 32, 66
monkeys 51
mosses 21, 48
moths 51, 55
mulberry 38
mythology 6–7, 11, 38
needles 10, 11, 30, 31, 71
nuthatches 21
nutmeg 42
nuts 40–43, 51, 71

O

oak 3, 6, 8, 14, 25, 27, 47, 50, 51, 59, 64
  cork 22
  English 8, 25, 33
  sessile 67

olives 39
oranges 39
orchids 21

PQ

palm 7, 12, 13, 32, 42, 43, 64, 67
  African raffia 64
  chusan 67
  coconut 67
  talipot 64
papaya 43
paper 65
parasites 21, 71
pear 4, 25
Persian ironwood 46
pests 55
petrified wood 48
photosynthesis 71
pine martens 50
pines 4, 10, 30, 31, 33, 45, 51
  bristlecone 16, 64, 65
  lodgepole 3, 53
  Scots 4, 10, 11, 45
  stone, 66
  sugar 45
  Weymouth 2, 45
plane 25, 27, 33, 41, 54
plums 2, 39
poisonous fruit 38, 40, 41
pollarding 61, 68, 71
pollen 32, 33, 36, 71
pollination 8, 32–37, 71
pollution 54–55, 64
poplar 25, 26
products, non-timber forest 63
pruning 60, 71
quinine 22

R

rabbits 19
rainforest 12, 13
redwood 16, 22, 30, 31, 64, 65
reforestation 62
religion 6, 11
resin 10, 23, 65
robinia 28
root caps 19
root hairs 19
rootlets 14, 15, 18, 19
roots 6, 12, 14, 17, 18–19, 71
  breathing 18
  pillar 13, 65
  stilt 18
rowan 2, 4, 28, 36, 38
rubber 22

ST

sap 20, 71
sapwood 16, 17, 48, 71
sawing 56–57
scales 10, 30–31
scent 31, 34, 36, 37
seasons 12, 30, 46, 47
seed cases 14
seedlings 14–15, 53 71
seeds 14, 38–43, 71
sequoia 6, 17, 31, 44, 53, 64, 65
sloths 51
softwood 58, 71
spices 42
spruce 10, 11, 30, 31, 44
  Norway 10
squirrels 20, 41
sumac 18, 31
swamps 18, 31
sycamore 3, 16, 36, 46, 51
tamarind 42
temperate zone 17, 19, 68
thuja 31
timber 56, 57, 63, 65
toads, 52
toadstools 49
treecreepers 20
tree-ferns 7, 13
tropical zone 12, 13, 18, 42, 43
trunk 6, 16, 20, 21, 71
tulip 27, 37, 41, 47
turning 59

VWY

veneers 57
walnut 28, 33, 57, 58
wasps 50
wayfaring 25
weather 52, 53
weeping fig 12
weevils 21, 51
wellingtonia 4, 6, 16, 17, 23, 31, 44
wildfires 52–53
willow 2, 14, 26, 50, 61
  dwarf 16
wind pollination 32
wing-nut 28, 40
witch's brooms 24
wood 48, 56–57, 71
  uses 58–59, 69
woodlice 48
worms 19
yew 10, 16, 23, 30, 32, 38, 54, 58, 64, 65, 66
Yggdrasil 6

Acknowledgments

The author and Dorling Kindersley would like to thank: the curator and staff, Westonbirt Arboretum; Simon White of the Botanic Gardens, Bath; Linda Gamlin; George Wiltshire; Forestry Commission; Alice Holt Lodge; and Marika Rae for their advice and help in supplying specimens for photography. Mark Ricks Tree Services of Bath for supplying and transporting the large specimens. Ken Day for supplying sawn sections and prepared timbers. Arthur Chater, Caroline Whiteford, Gary Summons and Chris Owen at the Natural History Museum. Ray Owen for artwork. Gabrielle Bamford for typing. Ashwin Khurana for text editing.

Illustrations by: Coral Mula; Mick Loates and David More of Linden Artists.

Picture research by: Millie Trowbridge.

Picture credits:
The publisher would like to thank the following for their kind permission to reproduce their photographs:

Key: a=above, t=top, b=bottom, m=middle, l=left, r=right.
Alamy Images: Roger Fletcher 65c. Heather Angel: 18b; 61b. Arboretum national des Barres: 69br. BPCC/Aldus Archive: 7b, 12ml, r; 22t; 45t. BTCV: Dave Donohue 68tr. Chris Beetles Ltd: 10m. G I Bernard/Oxford Scientific Films: 24mr. Bridgeman Art Library/Bonhams: 6bl. Dr Jeremy Burgess/Science Photo Library: 32b. Jane Burton/Bruce Coleman Ltd: 24ml. Robert Burton/Bruce Coleman Ltd: 48m. Jim Clare/Partridge Films Ltd/OSF: 20ml, mr. Eric Crichton/Bruce Coleman Ltd: 32m; 36m. Corbis: Robert Estall 64bl; Eric and David Hosking 66cra; Paul A Souders 67clb; Markow Tatiana 65clb. Stephen Dalton/NHPA: 21mb. 2 Deane/Bruce Coleman Ltd: 21t. Mansell Collection: 19b; 41b; 53t. Mary Evans Picture Library: 6br; 12t; 23t; 37m; 38t; 43mr; 51m, br; 56tl; 57t; 59t; 60t; 62t. Fine Art Photographic Library: 8m; 11b. Jeff Foott / Bruce Coleman Ltd: 51t. John Freeman: 56tr. Linda Gamlin: 16tl. David Grewcock/Frank Lane: 48tr. Brian Hawkes/NHPA: 16b. Michael Holford: 6t; 58t. Eric and David Hosking: 16mr; 21 tm. E A James/NHPA: 9mr. J Koivula/Science Source: 23m. Frank Lane: 16ml; 50ml. R P Lawrence / Frank Lane: 24b. Laura Lushington/ Sonia Halliday Photographs: 42r. John Mason/Ardca: 49m. G A Mather/Robert Harding: 16tr. G J H Moon/Frank Lane: 9ml. M Newman/Frank Lane: 48tl. Oxford Scientific Films: David Cayless 68crb; John Gerlach / AA 65bc; Ronald Toms 68bl. Fritz Prensel/Bruce Coleman Ltd: 13t. Photos Horticultural: 64tr, 65tr. Hans Reinhard/Bruce ColemanLtd: 19r; 21b; 50mr. Silvestris/Frank Lane: 54. Still Pictures: Paul Harrison 69tl. Kim Taylor/Bruce Coleman Ltd: 53b; 55. Roger Tidman/Frank Lane: 61m. Rodger Tidman/NHPA: 14. Norman Tomalin/Brucc Coleman Ltd: 18m. L West/Frank Lane: 46. Christian Zuber/ Bruce Coleman Ltd: 42ml. Corbis: Marnie Burkhart 53cla; Warren Faidley 52tl; Louie Psihoyos 53tl; Kevin Schafer 63br; Scientifica/Visuals Unlimited 55tl. Dreamstime.com: Dtfoxfoto 63t; Henrikhl 55cr; Skylightpictures 52b; Vasilis Ververidis 52-53t; Peter Wollinga 63cb. Getty Images: Romeo Gacad/AFP 62b. Glowimages: Malcolm Schuyl/ FLPA 62tr.

All other images © Dorling Kindersley
For further information see: www.dkimages.com